The Isle of Purbeck
in Pen and Ink
by
Roy Carr

HALSGROVE

First published in Great Britain in 2018

Copyright © Roy Carr 2018

British Library Cataloguing-in-Publication Data
A CIP record for this title is available from the British Library

ISBN 978 0 85704 308 5

HALSGROVE
Halsgrove House,
Ryelands Industrial Estate,
Bagley Road, Wellington, Somerset TA21 9PZ
Tel: 01823 653777   Fax: 01823 216796
email: sales@halsgrove.com

Part of the Halsgrove group of companies
Information on all Halsgrove titles is available at: www.halsgrove.com

Printed and bound by Parksons Graphics, India

Dedication

This book is for my son
ROBERT
A Dorsetman Born and Bred

Contents

Bibliography

R.C.H.M.	Dorset - Volume II, Parts 1,2,3.	1970
Paul Hyland	Purbeck - The Ingrained Island	1978
Rodney Legg	Corfe Castle Encyclopedia	2000
Arthur Mee	Dorset - The King's England	1967
Cecil N. Cullingford	A History of Dorset	1980
Jo Draper	Dorset, the Complete Guide	1986
Rodney Legg	The Jurassic Coast	2002
Rodney Legg	Witches of Dorset	1974
A. D. Mills	Dorset Place Names	1998
Jo Thomas	Discover Dorset - Stone Quarrying	1998
Harry & Hugh Ashley	The Dorset Village Book	1984
Jeremy Harte	Discover Dorset - Legends	1998

Introduction

The sturdy Island of Purbeck, just 14 miles by 9, lies in the southern part of Dorset and reflects the county as an area of inordinate beauty and variety.

The name derives from the Anglo-Saxon words 'pur' and 'bic' meaning 'beak shaped ridge frequented by Bitterne or Snipe' and, though carrying the title, it is not in truth an island. With stretches of water on three sides, Poole Harbour to the north and the English Channel to the east and south, it comes close. However, the western boundary is defined only by the tiny stream called Luckford Lake, a tributary of the River Frome.

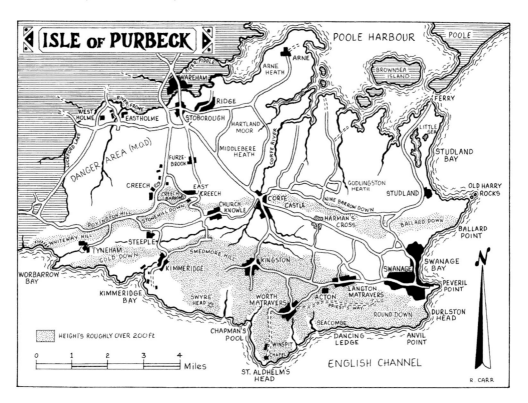

ISLE of PURBECK

HEIGHTS ROUGHLY OVER 200 ft

R. CARR

In ancient times, when marshland extended high up the river valley, Purbeck would have appeared as an island in the true sense. When winter gales flood the water-meadows beyond Wareham, the visitor can gain an impression of how it would have appeared in past times and, with global warming, how it could look in the future. Despite these anomalies, Purbeck is an island in a unique way. Its history, character and insular identity were best described by the author Paul Hyland who called it "... an island of the mind."

There are four ways to gain vehicular access to Purbeck of which three are open all year round.

Entry via Wareham's South Bridge, or round the town by-pass is the most frequented. A lesser known route is by a small road from East Holme to Stoborough.

From Lulworth Castle, a scenic route takes you across Whiteway and Povington hills. However, this road passes through the military firing ranges and access is

South Bridge and causeway at Wareham

restricted for a substantial part of the year. The best, and most impressive route is by the chain ferry which crosses the narrow Poole Harbour entrance between Sandbanks and South Haven. Although, at the height of the holiday season you must be prepared for a lengthy queue, this short voyage heightens the impression of landing on an island

Whatever the chosen route, the visitor enters a landscape of purple heathland backed by rolling hills and sheltered valleys, a place steeped in a history of conflict, murder, smugglers and poaching. The coastline, now a World Heritage Site, varies from the secretive inlets of Poole Harbour to the sandy, dune-fringed beaches of Studland which ascend onto the chalk cliffs of Handfast Point.

The road up Whiteway Hill

Further west, beyond the popular holiday resort of Swanage, huge limestone crags, pitted with quarry caves, offer dramatic coastal views. The cliffs turn to chalk, then descend to a stretch of the oldest Purbeck rock, the oil-bearing Kimmeridge shale, a dark and greasy stone. Inland, the island is bisected by a long, grass-covered ridge with only four road crossing points, the major gap housing a hill surmounted by the imposing ruins of Corfe Castle.

North of the ridge lie the heathlands dotted by old clay pits, many of which have flooded to become picturesque ponds, the most famous being the Blue Pool. High quality clay is still extracted from a quarry at Furzebrook from where it is dispatched to Staffordshire potteries.

It is however the north-eastern part of the heath that generates the greatest wealth for modern day Purbeck.

Sandbanks to Studland ferry

Amidst the heather and forestry plantations lies the unseen industrial machinery which pumps high grade oil to the surface. Under the general heading of Wytch Farm, it is the largest onshore oilfield in Britain. To the credit of the managing company, who work closely with conservation organisations, most of the plant is well concealed, leaving virtually unspoiled countryside on view. South of the central ridgeway runs the long valley which culminates at the coastal town of Swanage. Within its bounds lie most of the farms on the island. Agriculture revolves around the growing of oil-seed rape and cereal crops amid many other fields where cattle and sheep are grazed.

Between 1212 AD and 1615 AD, Purbeck was a Royal hunting ground and thus subject to 'Forest Laws'. Because of the lack of large wooded areas, it was generally referred to as the 'King's Warren' and retains, even today, a large population of deer, hare and rabbit. All came under the jurisdiction of the Constable of Corfe Castle. Poaching was, and still is, rife, and carried the most severe punishments if caught. Permission had to be obtained from the Constable to cut timber, build walls, create hedges or even to allow a daughter to marry anyone from outside of the Island.

CORFE CASTLE

South of the valley, hillsides rise to a maximum height of 500 feet before terminating on the rugged cliffs of the Jurassic Coast.

Beneath the surface of this high ground lies Purbeck's other famous natural resource - stone. This windswept plateau of marble is scarred by man's mining endeavours, carried out since Roman times. The pick and drill frequently unearth secrets of an even more ancient landscape - the fossils, footprints and trails left by dinosaurs and preserved for eternity in the mellow rock.

To the south and west of Kingston village, the terrain presents a slightly gentler aspect. Here, in secluded valleys are situated two of the great houses on the island, Encombe and Smedmore, the latter lying close to the picturesque village of Kimmeridge above its bay of black shale.

Further west, and nestling at the head of the Corfe River valley is the ruined 'ghost village' of Tyneham. This once bustling community, with its manor house, was cleared of its inhabitants in 1943 when the Ministry of Defence took the land for use as part of a live-firing range. Despite hollow promises, the area was never returned to the people and remains a training ground. With red flags denoting its boundaries, public access to this large part of Purbeck is prohibited except for those occasions, usually at weekends and holidays, when the military condescend to allow use of designated roads and footpaths.

Despite the intrusions of quarrymen, clay-cutters, army and oil companies, Purbeck remains a place of staggering beauty and tranquillity, a fact borne out by the thousands of tourists who come to the island each year. For both visitors and local people, it is a source of interest and mystery, a place where a person can stretch their legs whilst discovering new and secret niches within its bounds.

To stroll through Purbeck is not only a journey across exhilarating surroundings, but also a walk through history.

Studland

When entering the Isle of Purbeck via the Sandbanks Ferry you disembark at South Haven Point, the northernmost tip of Shell Bay and the Studland peninsula.

For those intrepid walkers with enough dedication and stamina, this is also the starting point of the South West Coastal Path. This 630 mile long and arduous route follows the shoreline through Dorset, Devon and Cornwall before ending at Minehead in Somerset.

The Shell Café

If your fancy is for a more leisurely lifestyle, just across the road is the famous Shell Café. Not surprisingly, this fine establishment specialises in seafood and offers excellent views across Poole Harbour.

A few yards up the road, you will reach a set of toll gates, not for admission to the way ahead, but to pay for your ferry crossing. To the right is an area called Bramble Bush Bay, bleak and bordered by mud flats.

The Toll Gates

Here can be found traces of over seventy circles, mounds and standing stones, thought to date from the Bronze or Iron Age.

The road continues between Studland Heath and the lagoon known as Little Sea and it is two miles before you come to the first substantial building, the Knoll House Hotel.

Surrounded by heathland, hills and cliffs, together with 3 miles of glorious beaches, Studland has given rise to a wealth of holiday accomodation. Though it does not cater for caravans or camping, there are cottages to rent and three very good hotels.

Pleasantly sited on the edge of the heath and close to the beach, the Knoll House Hotel has a high reputation for its friendly, family orientated atmosphere. With local strong associations with the authors H.G. Wells, Thomas Hardy and Enid Blyton. I particularly like the description by one guest who said their stay was like -

".. a return to Neverland".

Built during the 19th century by the Rt. Hon. George Bankes of Kingston Lacey, the Manor House Hotel incorporates features which date back to 1750.

It has a haphazard, romantic appearance with turrets, towers and mock battlements, The inspiration was based on the questionable belief that it was built on the site of the medieval Studland Castle.

Manor House Hotel

Over the years it has been enlarged and modernised and, in 2014, the name was changed to "The Pig on the Beach". Now painted a bright yellow, it has been themed in the 'shabby-chic' style' in vogue at the time.

A very popular Inn, fronted by a large garden, the creeper-clad Bankes Arms is reputed to have once been the haunt of smugglers.

Serving good food and a selection of Real Ales it incorporates the Isle of Purbeck Brewery and is noted for its annual beer festival held during August.

Bankes Arms

Situated in the village, it offers excellent accomodation and good access to South Beach.

Situated just below the Knoll House Hotel is the centre of the National Trust's stewardship of Studland's beaches. Backed by nearly 2 miles of sand dunes, Knoll Beach offers the finest view of the bay. With a restaurant, shop, toilet block and sailing centre, it is very popular with holidaymakers.
The gently sloping beach is safe for bathing and water sports but, be aware that a

Studland Bay from Knoll Beach

section is designated for the use of nudists so look for the warning signs. The bay also contains a protected area of shallow water containing sea grass meadows. These are the breeding grounds for the endangered Spiny and Short Tailed seahorses.

Discovery Centre

Above the spacious car park is the ecologically built Discovery and Field Study Centre. Besides catering for educational requirements, it also serves as a meeting place of the Purbeck Association of the National Trust. The area is an excellent starting point for many of the walks around the Studland countryside.

One excellent trailway from the Discovery Centre leads along the peninsula passing Little Sea. This mile long lake has evolved over the last four centuries, for Camden's map of 1607 shows that it did not exist at that time. However, deposits of sand caused a steady build up of the dunes which isolated this stretch of water. By 1785 it was depicted as a lagoon with an opening to the sea, a gap which gradually closed.

Nowadays it is a freshwater lake inhabited by small fish, newts and toads which, in turn, attract ducks, cormorants, herons, otters and other birds of prey. The shoreline is now the domain of shrews, mice and reptiles, all of which have resulted in a much visited Nature Reserve.

Little Sea

Middle Beach lies at the northern fringe of the village down an approach road which passes by some attractive thatched cottages.

Middle Beach and Café

Reached down a set of steps, the beach is sandy with outcrops of rock. It offers excellent views of Handfast Point and Old Harry Rocks.

Facilities include toilets and one of the best known cafés on Purbeck, good food and a barbecue area. Beyond are several rows of stilted beach huts amongst low dunes. At its southern end, the beach becomes rocky and terminates against a cliff called Redend Point. Carved by the elements, this tree-shrouded buttress is reddish-brown in colour and streaked with crimson and yellow sandstone.

The point can only be rounded at low tide when care must be taken as the rocks are slippery and there is a risk of falling debris.

Redend Point

In 1984, divers discovered a wreck in the bay. Originally thought to be the remains of the 'San Salvador' a warship of the Spanish Armada, it is more likely that it was an armed cargo ship, the 'Santa Maria de Luce' of the same period.

South Beach

South Beach is the smallest on Studland but this sandy cove has a friendly atmosphere and is ideal for children. There is a line of beach huts above a stone breakwater and a pleasant café. A little more sheltered than the other beaches, it provides a good mooring spot for visiting pleasure craft.

Many reviews declare it to be,
"the best beach on Studland".

During World War II, Studland, with its long stretch of beaches was considered a likely landing place for an invasion. Remains of its defensive system can be found all over the peninsula and South Beach is no exception. At the northern end, leaning rather drunkenly against the cliff at Redend Point is a Grade II listed, Type 25, pill-box. Nearby, a path ascends through dense trees to the top of the cliff and the largest wartime building on Purbeck.

In the autumn of 1943, Studland had become the training area for amphibious landings in preparation for D-Day. The 60 foot long Fort Henry was built as an observation post from which to watch the rehearsals.

Pill-box at Redend Point

In April 1944, it received its most notable visitors which included King George VI, Winston Churchill with Generals Montgomery and Eisenhower. They must have been satisfied as, two months later, the landings took place in Normandy. Behind the blockhouse lie the remains of a 6 inch gun emplacement.

LCVP

Fort Henry

Ever since the early 15th century, Studland had the reputation of being a lawless area "infested by pirates and smugglers". The bay offered a

safe anchorage and a quick escape route without having to run the gauntlet of the Preventive Officers at the narrow entrance to Poole Harbour. The inhabitants of the village were also involved, permitting the sale of contraband at 'markets' on the beach. They also provided entertainment for the seamen through inns and houses of ill repute - the most notorious being the cottages of Joan Chaddock, Roger and William Munday in Watery Lane.

Goods destined to go inland were stored in local barns, caves and under piles of seaweed which had been harvested as fertilizer. Other cargoes were transported across the heaths to small piers as Goathorn and Ower from where they were shipped to Poole.

Cottages in Watery Lane
(From a photograph taken in 1895)

Barn at Manor House Farm
(Once a hideaway for smuggled goods.)

One famous seafaring adventurer operating in the area was Henry (Harry) Paye of Poole. Pirate, smuggler and wrecker, the authorities eventually recognised his talent and made him a Commander of the Cinque Ports.

During the Elizabethan era, rival gangs of smugglers carried out their trade - with no love lost between them, none more so than those led by John Piers and Clinton Atkinson. Piers and his gang were eventually captured, tried, most oddly, by their rivals, and sentenced to death. They were held in Corfe Castle from where they were taken to Studland and hung in chains below the high water mark.

There can be little doubt that the local gentry were in league with the smugglers and several became wealthier through their association. This was highlighted by the fact that Atkinson was godson to the Earl of Lincoln, Lord Admiral of England. Clinton suffered the same fate as Piers and, together with five of his gang, was convicted and executed at Wapping. Their deaths had no effect on the trade, for smuggling remained rife in Studland throughout the following centuries.

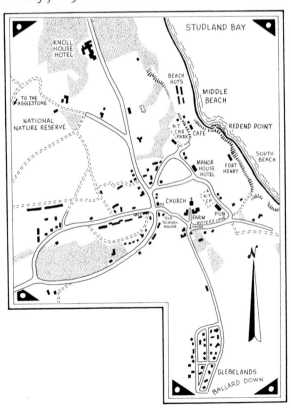

Village Hall

The tree-shrouded village of Studland nestles comfortably below Ballard Down. Sometimes described as a "miniature seaside town", it is mainly Edwardian in style, but retains many older cottages and buildings.

A cross roads at the entrance to the village is flanked by the Post Office cum stores and the Community Hall. Always busy, they are the places to catch up on the latest news and gossip.

Opposite stands the new Village Hall. Built in 2006, it boasts excellent facilities.

The Old School

Post Office and Stores

A short distance down School Lane, to the right of the Post Office is, not surprisingly, the Old Schoolhouse.

As well as catering for the education of the village children, it was also the home to the teacher.

It was in use from 1840 until the early 1950s and now serves as a very pretty holiday cottage.

The writer Virginia Woolf lived in Studland for four years from 1909 until 1913 where, with visiting friends of the 'Bloomsbury Set, she became the source of many a village scandal.

Another author, Enid Blyton, was a frequent visitor to Studland.

In her 'Noddy' series of books, she based the character 'Mr Plod the Policeman' on Christopher Rone, the local 'Bobby' at that time.

The centre of the old part of the village is situated where School Lane meets Watery Lane. It is marked by a large grassy mound surmounted by a beautiful carved cross. The original cross, of local heathstone, was erected in Saxon times but, of this, only the circular plinth remains. The present version was sculpted in Purbeck Marble and placed here in 1976. The carving was carried out by local mason Trevor Heysom whose design and symbolism is astounding. Almost every inch of the stone is covered in motifs representing ancient history, art, modern life, religion, science and nature to armed conflict. A visit to Studland would not be complete without a study of this wonderful piece of sculpture.

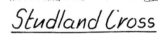

Studland Cross

Cart Shelter

Close to the foot of the mound is a rare, open building of stone and thatch, once used, it is thought, as a cart shelter.

In times past, the cross was also the site for public humiliation as, until 1850, the village stocks stood beside it.

A few yards up the lane to the church, Studland Manor Farmhouse and its barn is quite impressive. The house was built in two stages, which is plainly evident. The upper storey is of brick, thought to have been added in the early 18th century, whilst the ground floor and manor are older and have walls of rubble. Victorian in style, the cross wing to the south was added during the late 19th century.

Manor Farmhouse

The original farm cottage is now a private dwelling.

Opposite, the large barn is also of the 1700s and built of rubble and brick.

As with its counterparts at Worth and Arne, the parish church at Studland is dedicated to St Nicholas of Myra, the patron saint of sailors. Just by the manor, and set within Yew trees, it is an almost perfect example of Norman architecture.

Church of St Nicholas

The original church was built pre-conquest and some of its Saxon stonework remains woven into the north wall.

When being constructed in the 11th century, it was discovered that the foundations were not strong enough to support the Norman concept of a tall tower. Therefore the builders had to leave it unfinished and capped the bell-storey with a saddle roof, leaving the rather squat appearance we see today.

The porch was added in the 17th century and the east window is in the Early English style. The beautiful interior has a superb Norman arch and the plain font is thought to be older than the church itself. Where walls meet the roof on the outside, there is a fascinating Corbel table decorated with carvings of grotesque faces and animals.

Corbel Table

'Saxon' Font

Just by the porch is a double-sided gravestone recording the life of Studland's most celebrated soldier, Sergeant William Lawrence, of the 40th Regiment of Foot.

Having served in South America, he joined the Duke of Wellington's army in Portugal during the Napoleonic Wars. He fought in most of the Peninsular battles, including the particular bloody storming of Badajoz where he was severely wounded.   He recovered enough to take part in the decisive battle of Vittoria and, eventually, was in charge of the regimental colour at Waterloo.   He married a French girl, Clothilde Clairet, and returned to Studland where they ran a pub called 'The Wellington'. Buried in the same grave, Clothilde's epitaph is engraved, in French, on the reverse of the stone.

Grave of the Dorset Soldier

Godlingston Heath is a National Nature Reserve which stretches north from the slopes of Ballard Down.

It is an internationally important lowland heath, listed as a Site of Special Scientific Interest (SSSI). All six species of British reptiles can be found here together with a plethora of bird life, including the rare Dartford Warbler.

Godlingston Heath

Balanced on a conical sandhill, the Agglestone stands uniquely amid an expanse of heather and gorse. This 500 ton, 18 foot high, vividly coloured block of Ironstone has attracted visitors for hundreds of years. Some thought it to be a monolith set up by Stone or Bronze-Age man, whilst the Victorians believed it was a huge Druid altar. It is, in fact, completely natural, uncovered by centuries of erosion. However, it is so striking that it deserves to warrant a Purbeck legend, which I prefer. The Devil used to perch atop the Needles, on the Isle of Wight, waiting for lost souls. One clear, cold night, he awoke to see the ramparts of Corfe Castle silhouetted against the moon. This beautiful sight so enraged Satan that he tore off his nightcap and hurled it towards the offending fortress.

The Agglestone

Though his aim was true, he lacked in strength and the cap fell short, to land on the heath where it turned into a stone outcrop, the Agglestone of Studland.

Throughout the centuries, other names for the rock have included 'Hagstone', 'Holystone' and 'Witches-stone'.

The tassel on the nightcap came off with the impact and landed 400 yards to the north where it turned into the Puckstone. Overgrown with gorse and fern, it is a little difficult to locate but can be found on a small hillock just off the main track.

The Puckstone

Beyond the village, the Coastal Path rises gently to the most easterly cape on Purbeck, Handfast Point. Below is one of the most iconic features of the isle, the isolated chalk stacks known as 'Old Harry Rocks'. They are named after the Devil who had taken up residence in caves below the cliffs, an area appropriately titled 'Old Nick's Ground'. Once there was another stack, 'Old Harry's Wife', but it collapsed into the sea in 1896.

The Pinnacles

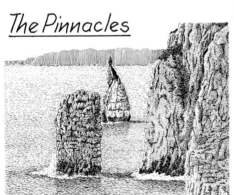

Handfast Point and Old Harry Rocks

Fishermen used to shelter in the caves during winter as they were always warm, due, legend has it, to the fires of hell, created within by the Devil.
One huge cavern named 'Parsons Barn' was once a hiding place for smuggled goods, but it has now been claimed by the sea.

Overlooking and encroaching upon Godlingston Heath is the Isle of Purbeck Golf Club. Founded in 1892, it commands breathtaking views over Poole Harbour, the bay and as far as the Isle of Wight.

Golf Clubhouse

The writer Enid Blyton purchased the course from Harry Palmer in 1950 as a gift for her husband, Kenneth Waters, paying the princely sum of £1.

Ballard Down from Ulwell

From Handfast Point, the path leads along the edge of sheer cliffs, a pleasant walk which, in the right season, is pervaded with the tangy aroma of wild garlic.

Eventually, the going becomes a little steeper as you rise onto the ridgeway across the two-mile long Ballard Down.

This 162 metre high, grass covered whaleback of a hill is one of the largest areas of chalkland on Purbeck. A short way along its length, where a steep path rises from Swanage, a rectangular block of stone is a welcome place to take a break.

This 'rest and be thankful seat' was installed in 1852 by David Jardine, a Bow Street Magistrate and frequent visitor to Dorset. From the seat, a further mile along the ridgeway is an obelisk which marks the end of Ballard Down. Here, a path descends steeply into Ullwell Gap and out of the Studland parish.

Rest and be thankful seat

Ulwell

The Obelisk

Situated to the south of the Gap, Ulwell has been occupied for thousands of years. This is borne out by thousands of archeological finds of worked flint dating from 8,000 bc. King John built a hunting lodge nearby at Whitecliff Farm, remains of which can still be seen. The obelisk at the end of Ballard Down was erected by George Burt to celebrate the completion of a reservoir he built to supply water to Swanage.

As with many of his architectural objects installed in the area, it was recycled from a street corner in London.

It was dismantled during the early years of World War II as it was thought it could serve as a seamark for an enemy attack.

In 1973, it was rebuilt by 129 Field Squadron, Royal Engineers. During the operation, they found that the lower section had cracked, so this was mounted alongside the plinth.

The 20th century has seen Swanage expand into Ulwell, so much so that the village is considered to be part of the town. The modern era has also witnessed a change in farmland behind Ulwell Cottage. It has been developed into an award winning caravan site which incorporates the Village Inn, shop restaurant with excellent access paths to the surrounding hills.

Village Inn and shop

'Tall Trees'

A short distance down the road, by a footpath leading to Whitecliff Farm, stands a small cottage named 'Tall Trees'. Now a holiday let, the building dates from 1764, is Grade II listed as it once housed the village forge and stables.

Half a mile to the south-west of Ulwell, and bearing a name which has remained unchanged since Medieval times, Godlingston is the oldest manor on Purbeck. The original part of the house was built around 1300 AD and consisted of a tower and an attached rectangular building. Signs where the two parts meet suggest that it stands on the site of an earlier structure, perhaps a Saxon timber hall. The tower was probably used as a defensive refuge, for it has thick walls and no ground floor entrance. The manor was extended through the 17th and 18th centuries. During the Elizabethan era it was occupied by Henry Wells, a staunch Roman Catholic, who is thought to have used the tower as a safe haven for priests in those dangerous times.

A reservoir which served the property is shrouded in woodland just north of the house.

With an abutting farm and stables, Godlingston is noted for its annual horse-show based in the manor yard every August.

Godlingston Manor

Above Godlingston Manor, close by the summit of Kingswood Down, lies a rather sad memorial to the passage of time. With the advent of G.P.S., the old Ordnance Survey Triangulation Pillar fell into disuse. It has been toppled from its high point and now sits forlornly on the hillside.

THE WITCHES OF ULWELL

Purbeck, like many other regions, has its fair share of peculiar old ladies labelled 'witches' by neighbours. One such was Jinny Gould who lived in a cottage by the toll gate at Ulwell. As the keeper, it was rumoured that she was paid by the smugglers to leave the gate open at night so their passage would be unhindered. She was named as a witch because it was thought she could change into a large black cat which would sit on the gate, spitting and snarling at

travellers, hoping to terrify them. One such character was a carter, who was so furious at the animal that he struck it across the spine with his whip. With a terrible scream, the cat vanished into thin air. Next day, Jinny was found dead in her cottage with a great wound on her back. After her death, it is said that the gate would open of its own accord just in case the smugglers had to pass.

However, it is more common for local witches to have hares as their familiars. One night such a 'witch-hare' was spotted by a poacher on a hill above Ulwell. He quickly dealt it a heavy blow behind its ears with his stick. The wounded animal bounded away and disappeared into the garden of a cottage wherein dwelt Maria Gover, an ancient lady, suspected of being a witch. Within two days, old Maria had taken to her sick bed, and died. Isn't folklore wonderfully fascinating and scary!

Swanage

From Ulwell, the road descends through a residential area known as New Swanage onto the promenade of this popular holiday resort. To the east, the groyned beach, backed by steep cliffs, stretches along the foot of Ballard Down. The seafront is lined with dozens of beach huts at the end of which stairways lead to the top of the cliffs, where hotels perch on the edge. Due to present changes in climate, these chalk precipices are gradually being eroded and rock falls are common.

Beach huts below New Swanage

Stone jetty

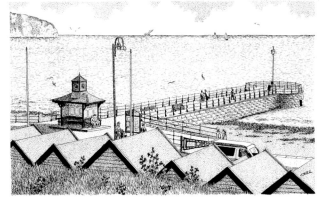

Westwards, the esplanade and Shore Road lead towards the town which, halfway along, the beach is broken by a shelter, surmounted by a clock, and a 60 foot long stone pier.
Built in 1992, this jetty was designed as an outlet for storm water that was causing winter flooding in the town.

Beyond the jetty, a line of modern beach huts lead into the more recreational part of the seafront. Shops, cafés, arcades, toilets and the Mowlem Theatre cluster round this end of the promenade.

Across Shore Road, a green hillock is topped by an amusement park, an amphitheatre containing a bandstand and, close by, the War Memorial.

Bandstand and War Memorial.

Close by the theatre is a rather misleading memorial column erected by John Mowlem in 1862. The inscription reads:- "In Commemoration of a Great Naval Battle fought with the Danes in Swanage Bay by Alfred the Great A.D. 877." In truth, there was no battle as the fleet of 120 Danish ships, on leaving Wareham to sail to Exeter, were caught in a storm and wrecked on the rocks off Peveril Point.

Oddly, the cannonballs on the top are relics from the Crimean War

King Alfred Column

During the busiest years of quarrying, the seafront at the foot of the High Street was very different to what is seen now. Stone would be hauled from the quarries to the shoreline between the Swan Brook and Pitt's stone quay to await shipment. Tall heaps of dressed stone called 'Bankers' were deposited at the various merchants' allotted areas. The blocks were then loaded onto horse-drawn, high-wheeled carts and taken down the slipway where they were hoisted aboard lighters.

These shallow, flat bottomed craft would ferry the stone to bigger boats in deeper water on which it was transported to London. This long process made for arduous and backbreaking work and was not a very efficient system.

In an effort to speed up the operation, the builder John Mowlem founded the Swanage Pier and Tramway Company. His plan was to carry the stone by rail from the quarries at Langton Matravers to his new pier, built in 1859. Due to local opposition, the tramway was never completed, but some of the rails can be seen embedded in the seafront close to the slipway.

Tramway rails and 'Coal Depot'

A long, low building by the tramway, possibly intended as a Coal Depot, became a fish store to which catches were hauled along the rails. Eventually the shed was used as an indoor market but now houses the Museum and Heritage Centre.

Museum/Heritage Centre

When the railway came to Swanage in 1885, it became quicker to transport stone by train and the 'Bankers' were no longer needed.

With the advent of tourism, the site was developed into a long terrace of elegant houses and renamed 'The Parade'.

The Parade (Site of the 'Bankers')

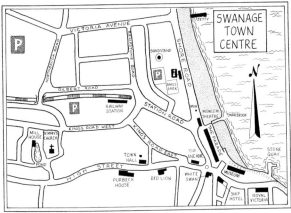

The Church of Saint Mary lies at the heart of the oldest part of the original village of 'Swanwick'. Its only medieval structure is the sturdy West Tower which dates from the 14th century, though some earlier stonework is evident in some of the walls.

St Mary's Church

The tower was heightened in 1620 when most of the church was rebuilt. Completion of the building took place in the 19th century and further enlargement carried out in 1907. During its lifetime, the tower did duty as a soldiers lookout and is believed to have been used by villagers as a refuge from raiding pirates. Amongst many church memorials, a simple plaque above the vestry door commemorates Chief Petty Officer Ernest Pitcher, Swanage's only holder of the Victoria Cross.

Close by the church is a picturesque mill pond surrounded by the loveliest group of cottages in the town, all built of local stone. The pond is fed by an unseen spring and bordered by a low stone wall built by John Mowlem to stop cattle from polluting the water.

The Mill Pond

Unsurprisingly, at its foot, where the pond is drained by a stream, stands a mill-house bearing the inscription:-
"BEn Barlow Millwright of Southampton fecit 1754."
Further up the hill, a cottage displays a plate stating that the preacher John Wesley spent a night there in 1774. This part of the town is a favourite spot for artists and photographers and not to be missed by visitors.

Mill House

Town Hall

One of the main features on the High Street has to be the Town Hall. Built by George Burt in 1882-3, it stands on the site of old almshouses in an area once known as 'The Drong'. Once the porch of the Mercer's Hall in London's Cheapside, the elaborate frontage was designed in 1670 by Edward Jerman, a student of Christopher Wren. One critic, on viewing the building, described it as a fine example of...
.....*"How to murder Architecture".*

The 'House of Confinement' or 'Lock-up' stands in a paved area behind the Town Hall. It was sometimes called the 'Blind House' as it had only one tiny window. An inscription above the iron studded door reads:- *"Erected for the prevention of Vice and Immorality by the Friends of Religion and good Order A.D. 1803".* It originally stood beside the church.

The 'Lock-up'

Purbeck House

A few yards up the High Street, across the road from the Town Hall, Purbeck House was bought by George Burt in 1875. He demolished the original Georgian building and remodelled it to suit Victorian tastes. His new house was built in a Scottish Baronial style resembling a rather bizarre castle and incorporated some features of the Royal castle of Balmoral. The house also contains many items salvaged from London including a tiled floor from the House of Commons. In 1935, Purbeck House was acquired by Roman Catholic nuns, the Sisters of Mercy who enhanced the quality of life by caring for the sick, poor, handicapped and elderly. They remained there for over 50 years, after which the house was developed into a rather elegant hotel.

At the height of the stone industry, Swanage harbour was an extremely busy and industrious place. Stone is heavy, and for those employed in the trade, the working hours were long and, for all involved, it was strenuous and exhausting toil. At the end of a day's labour, there was little to offer the workers as relaxation other than a pint of ale in the pub. Together with seamen off the waiting vessels, this made for a large and thirsty clientelle and the business of supplying liquor flourished. Therefore, it is not surprising that, right behind the 'Bankers', within a stretch of 150 yards of the High Street were four inns. They are all still trading, though nowadays, their customers tend to consist mainly of visitors seeking refreshment.

White Swan
A friendly, traditional pub in rustic style with a secluded walled garden.

The Anchor Inn
Claiming to be the oldest pub in Swanage, it is mainly used by a local clientelle and has a quiet, austere atmosphere with no outside seating.

Red Lion
This 19th century coach house specialises in real ales and accomodation. It has a large garden with a patio and covered, heated marquee. It is the only pub with on site parking.

The Ship Inn
Serves quality foods from local suppliers, has a garden and is noted for its annual Jazz and Blues festivals.

SWANAGE RAILWAY

In 1885, the railway came to Purbeck, running from Wareham, through Corfe Castle to terminate at Swanage. Besides carrying passengers, its primary function was to transport stone up to the main line.

However, in the early 20th century, seaside holidays became the trend and the number of visitors using the train increased. The line became so popular that, by 1931, demand required thirteen trains daily.

Sadly, due to Government cuts, the service came under the axe and the route was closed in 1972.

Later that year however, a group of enthusiastic volunteers founded the Swanage Railway Society with the aim of re-establishing their railway. They did not have much to start with - a boarded up station with no platforms or track. Depending entirely on volunteers and funding from donations, they began to work miracles. Within seven years they had laid new track, restored locomotives and, in 1982, Swanage station was officially re-opened.

Steam Locomotive 'Manston'

By 1993, the connection to Norden was finished and the project has now evolved into one of Britain's best preserved heritage railways. In 2016, the final track was laid to Wareham and the trains will soon be able to join the main line between London and Weymouth.

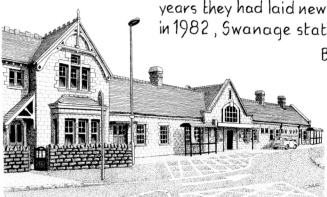

Swanage Station and Bus Depot

Riding these lovely steam trains is to take a journey through time, meandering from medieval ruins across the beautiful Purbeck countryside to the seashore amusements of Victorian Swanage.

Main Platform, Swanage Station

Water Tower and Signals

Westward from the Parade, the seafront makes for a very pleasant stroll. The first feature encountered is the old stone jetty with its panoramic views across the bay. Here you will find an excellent open air café with plenty of outside seating and specialising in fresh seafood.

Stone Jetty

Royal Victoria Hotel

Across the road stands a large, cream coloured building with a double staircase. In 1823, this was built as the Manor House Hotel by William Morton Pitt in his efforts to promote Swanage as a holiday resort. It was re-named in 1833 as the Royal Victoria Hotel after the future Queen stayed there overnight. Now a Grade II listed building, it has been developed as residential flats.

Swanage Pier

At the end of the seafront is the entrance to Swanage Pier which caters for over 100,000 visitors each year. The town has had two piers, the first being built in 1859 by John Mowlem to ease the loading of stone into moored vessels. A steamer service was started by George Burt in 1874 but proved so popular that he decided that a larger pier was needed.

Therefore, a new one was constructed between 1895-97 and ran alongside the old pier, the rotting pilings of which can still be seen today.

Regular steamer services from the new pier operated until 1966 when it fell into disrepair and was closed. In 1993, the Swanage Pier Trust was founded to raise money for restoration and, due to their efforts, it was eventually re-opened. As well as being a wonderful place to visit, it has facilities for sailing, fishing and scuba diving. The Diving School, near the pier entrance is the oldest established one in Britain. Summer sailing trips have been resumed as have the cruises on the last sea-going paddle steamer, the 'Waverley'. Also Grade II listed, it won the award for 'Pier of the Year' in 2012.

Peveril Point is a promontory which forms the southern end of Swanage Bay. It was once known as 'Perilous Point' because of the dangerous, and mostly hidden, ledges which extend out to sea from its foot, the cause of many a shipwreck.

Peveril Point

National Coastwatch lookout post.

The eastern extremity of the headland is topped by the National Coastwatch Institution lookout post which commands a magnificent view to Old Harry Rocks and the Isle of Wight to the north-east and south to Durlston Head. This natural defensive position covers the approaches to the Solent and the rock hides tunnels which once connected gun emplacements of World War II.

Not for the first time the point had been put to this use for, in 1774, it supported a watchouse and battery of six guns. This, in turn superseded a magazine and cannons sited here in 1584.

Below the lookout, at the foot of the northern shoreline, is the Swanage Lifeboat Station. At the time of writing, a modern replacement is being built alongside the present boathouse and slipway.

Close by, a lovely terrace of white cottages once housed the men of the Coastguard Service on constant lookout for ships in distress or smugglers. Nowadays, as with many properties on Purbeck, they have been redeveloped as holiday homes.

Old Coastguard Cottages

A short walk from the point, towards the town, the road passes below a manicured, grassy slope, a part of Prince Albert Gardens. This parkland is dominated by Swanage's 'Greek Ruins', a paved amphitheatre with tiered, stone seating and two prominent columns. These pillars are actually replicas of the 2,400 years old Athena Polias which once adorned a London building.

The arena is a venue for entertainment including plays, jazz bands and morris dancers.

Prince Albert Gardens

Wellington Clock Tower

Between the lifeboat station and the pier, a slender, Gothic style clock tower stands on top of a massive stone sea wall. Surrounded by a modern development of Mediterranean type flats and houses, it has been a feature of the Swanage skyline for well over a century.

It was originally erected as a memorial to the Duke of Wellington and graced the southern end of London Bridge. After ten years, it was deemed a hazard to traffic and dismantled. The pieces were shipped to Swanage as ballast by George Burt.

He rebuilt it in the grounds of the Grosvenor Hotel and was eventually moved to its present site. Originally crowned with an elegant steeple, this was replaced by a cupola. The clock tower has a bit of a quirky mystery – for it lacks a clock! In this drawing, the tower can be seen behind the remains of the old pier.

Piles of the old Pier

Another piece of humour stands on the seafront nearby. A 'derelict' building shocks the visitor at this eyesore left within a setting of tidy surroundings.

However, a second look brings a smile to their faces when they realize it is a rather clever painting.

By the gates of Prince Albert Gardens, a road leads uphill to Durlston.

Durlston Castle
AND THE JURASSIC COAST

The 'Derelict' Building

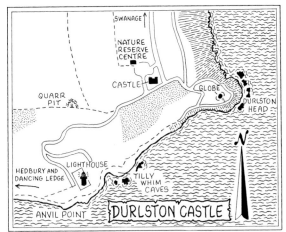

Durlston Castle was never constructed as a defensive position but was the vision of George Burt, the Victorian builder and benefactor of Swanage.

Durlston Castle

Built between 1887 and 1891, the castle stands within a landscape of elegant terraces with intersecting paths set amongst exotic trees and flowering shrubs. After Burt's death in 1894, Durlston passed through various ownerships until it was bought by the County Council in 1973 and the Nature Reserve and Countryside Park were created.

Originally built from local stone and supplemented by recycled artifacts from London, the castle has recently undergone a complete refurbishment. With a new restaurant, space for displays, exhibitions and entertainment, it has also been established as the 'gateway' and Information Centre for the Jurassic Coast. Entry from the car park is via a walled path which forms a timeline through the millennia. With an abundance of wildlife and amazing sea views, the paths lead the visitor on a walk amidst surroundings which are second to none.

The Great Globe

The Great Globe was another audacious enterprise of Burt. Carved from Portland stone in John Mowlem's yard at Greenwich in 1887, this ball, weighing 40 tons was inscribed with a map of the world and transported by sea to Purbeck in 15 segments. It was erected on a level platform, 136 feet above the sea to the south-east of the castle. Large stone plaques were set around it and inscribed with geographical and scientific data with quotes from Shakespeare, other poets and the Bible.

Close by are set eight granite blocks marking the points of the compass. Stone benches allow the visitor to relax within an atmosphere of peace, beauty, education and wonder at this inspiring and unique monument.

Anvil Point

Set within a walled compound, and gleaming white against the surrounding greenery, the picturesque lighthouse has stood on Anvil Point since 1881. Its chunky tower is 12 metres high and the light stands 45 metres above the high water mark. Originally lit by paraffin, the lamp was electrified in 1960 but is now fully automated and is operated from Harwich. The keepers are no longer required and their homes are now holiday cottages. The lighthouse is open to visitors at designated times.

On the hillside, above the lighthouse, a reconstructed 'quarr', (small underground quarry) is well worth a visit. Originally the capstan would be operated by a donkey tethered to the beam and walking in circles. This turned the windlass to bring the carts, loaded with stone, to the surface. Alongside there would have been an open-sided workshop and shelter known as a 'quarr-house' where the stone would be shaped and dressed.

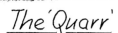

The 'Quarr'

Tilly Whim Quarry

Cut into the cliff between the castle and lighthouse are the ledges and galleries of Tilly Whim quarry which were mainly worked in the 18th century. The name 'Tilly' is that of a local quarryman whilst 'whim is the dialect word for the crane or winch which was used to lower the stone onto barges moored alongside the ledges.

When George Burt created the castle and park, he turned Tilly Whim quarry into a tourist attraction as 'caves'. For access, he had a doorway blasted into the tunnels and utilized a gate, railings and a stone pier from Pentonville Gaol in London. This entrance can be seen from the Coastal Path. Unfortunately, the cave system had to be closed in 1976 due to serious rockfalls and public access is no longer allowed. Nature has now reclaimed the site and the caves are the home to bats, whilst the cliffs support marine plants and nesting birds.

Cave Entrance

Here be Dinosaurs

The Jurassic Coast runs for 95 miles from Old Harry Rocks to Orcombe Point in East Devon. Established in 2001 by UNESCO, it is the only natural World Heritage Site in England, covering 185 million years of the Earth's history.

Footprints and fossils of dinosaurs, marine life, flora and fauna have been found on Purbeck for centuries where, initially they were regarded as witchcraft rather than science or history. One of the finest multiple dinosaur track sites was uncovered in 1997 at Keat's Quarry to the east of Worth Matravers.

Jurassic Coast above Dancing Ledge

In a report to the National Trust, Dr Jo Wright stated that the footprints had been made by at least twelve individual dinosaurs. With the continual erosion of the coast, it is almost guaranteed that future exciting discoveries will be made. Further west, the path passes above the gaping quarry caverns of Blackers Hole, only seen at their best from the sea. Inland from the cliffs, colonies of the rare Spider Orchid can be seen when in season. Beyond, the coastal path descends to one of Purbeck's favourite visitor spots....

Dancing Ledge

This large quarry, originally owned by the Hayward family is named after the action of the waves which appear to 'dance' across the flat shelf cut from the rock by quarrymen. At one time, the carts which laboured up the hill beyond carried a different cargo of 'hard-stuff' other than stone.

The ledge was a favourite landing spot used by gangs of smugglers bringing contraband ashore.

Towards the close of the 19th century, the headmaster of nearby Durnford boys school had a swimming pool blasted into the ledge for use by his pupils.

Nowadays this romantic, magical place is a popular spot for picnics and barbecues.

500 metres to the west, Hedbury quarry is a haven for rock climbers. This pretty little cove has a corroded 12 lb cannon mounted on a stone plinth, probably salvaged from one of the many wrecks off this coast.

Hedbury Cannon

Langton Matravers

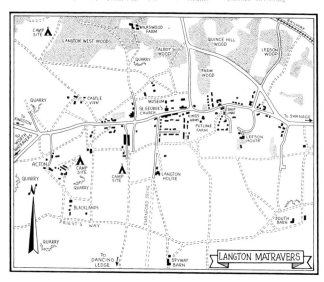

Situated just to the west of Swanage, Langton Matravers owed its medieval expansion to the stone trade and is the largest village on Purbeck associated with quarrying.

The name 'Langton' meaning 'long-farm' describes it perfectly, for it consists of one street nearly a mile in length.

Constructed almost entirely of local stone, few of its buildings are older than the 18th century.

High Street Cottages

The addition of Matravers to the name of the village came from the Mautravers family who became Lords of the Manor in the 13th century. One of its members, Sir John Mautravers, was implicated in the gruesome murder of King Edward II at Berkeley Castle in September 1327. Although strongly suspected, he was never formally accused.

High Street Cottages

Arms of the Mautravers Family

The King's Arms

Close to the centre of the village, the 'King's Arms' was named after George III who popularized the Dorset Coast, though he never visited Langton.
It was originally licensed in 1742 as the 'Mason's Arms' and refurbished during the 19th century when the porch was added.

Nearby, at the bottom of the High Street is Putlake Farm. Built in the 18th century, this cottage and barn were originally outbuildings of the larger Langton Manor Farm, across the road. Now independent, it is a working farm which has diversified into an 'Adventure' Centre for children. It offers a pet centre, go-karts, tractor rides and a maze, whilst the cottage is now a tea-room and shop.

Putlake Farm

Ship Inn

Beyond Putlake Farm, the road rises to Steps Hill, on the summit of which is the Ship Inn. The original alehouse opened in 1765 as a two storey cottage which was extended in later years.

In 1878, the landlord, John Ball, in a fit of depression, attempted to murder his wife Mary, after which he killed himself with the shotgun. As was the practice with suicides at that time, he was buried 'like a dog' outside the parish boundary.

This ritual so inflamed the rector, Rev. Lester Lester, that he successfully campaigned for a change in the law to allow churchyard funerals for suicides.

Leeson House

The site of Leeson House has been occupied since Saxon times and was recorded in Domesday Book as a farm called 'Lestington'. In 1805, the Rev. John Dampier demolished the farmhouse and built a new home which, during Victorian times was extended into its present form. In 1903 it was sold to a Miss Amy Blanche who established it as a boarding school for girls. During World War II, it was requisitioned by the Air Ministry after which it became a private school for boys. In 1967 it was re-established to become the principal Field Studies Centre for the Isle of Purbeck, and remains as such to this day. With accommodation for sixty students, it has a fully equipped laboratory, with seven acres of land, including three ponds, a bird hide and a small campsite.

Of all the churches on Purbeck, St George's of Langton has suffered most through incompetent rebuilding. Of the original 14th century church, only the battlemented tower remains. The nave was reconstructed in 1828, but, after only 45 years it had fallen into decay and was considered to be unsafe. The rector, Rev. Trotman declared it was "a disgrace to the Isle of Purbeck". Therefore, during 1875/6, the nave was rebuilt but its roofline was, oddly, higher than the tower. This may have been because it was planned to add a spire but, though designed, it was never built.

St. George's Church

The church warden to Rev. Trotman was Thomas Hayward who ran the quarry at Dancing Ledge and was also a notorious smuggler. One time he stored a large cargo of brandy in the roof space of the church. Unfortunately, during the following Sunday service, the ceiling gave way and the barrels bombarded the congregation, killing one of the worshippers.

In the graveyard stands a sculpture of a quarryman. It was created by noted sculptress Mary Spencer Watson who lived at nearby Dunshay Manor.

The Museum

Behind the church is a tiny museum housed in the former coach room of the rectory. Its fine exhibits bring to the visitor a complete picture of the hard life led by this rural community, especially in the way that the stone was quarried and used. With audio-visual presentation, photo's, tools, carvings, fossils and rebuilt quarry capstan, it is well worth a visit.

Rather surprisingly, for a village which owed its development to quarrying and the stone trade, by the late 19th and early 20th centuries the main industry in Langton was that of education. By 1929, there were no less than six schools established, including Leeson House.

Opposite the church, the village hall was originally a Weslyan Chapel, built in 1845. It incorporated the National School which provided a basic education for the children of the poor quarrymen and farmers.

St George's Primary

Village Hall

Built in 1870, St George's replaced the National School and catered for the teaching of all the village children. It remains as the primary school and, in 2014, a fully modernised expansion was completed.

Durnford House, built in 1725, became an academy for sons of gentlefolk in 1894 under headmaster Thomas Pellatt. It was a spartan, uncomfortable environment which included a daily 'strip' swim in the pool on Dancing Ledge. Occupied by radar scientists in WWII, it eventually became the private home of Lady Savage.

Durnford House

Close to the top of the village, this building was originally a brewery and alehouse called the 'Sweet Content'. In 1906, the school was founded there by Rex Corbett with just ten pupils. At its height in the '70s and '80s there were up to one hundred students but, by 2007, declining enrollment forced it to close. A year later it was bought by the Cothill Educational Trust as a science-based centre for schoolchildren aged between 10 and 13.

The Old Malthouse

Spyway School

Pellatt also built the imposing Langton House for his daughter Hester, who established Spyway School in the building, a preparatory for both boys and girls. During the 1970s, the house became a psychiatric unit for juveniles until it was bought by a holiday company in 1995 and refurbished into a grand hotel. The actor David Niven attended Spyway, whilst Durnford educated Ian Fleming, author of the James Bond books.

A lane which runs from the village past Langton House becomes a track known as Durnford Drove.
This path ascends to cross the Priest's Way, past Spyway Barn to terminate above Dancing Ledge.

Durnford Drove

At the bottom of a dead-end lane, just to the west of Langton, is the isolated hamlet of Acton.
First recorded in Domesday Book (1086) as the manor of 'Tacatone', it stands amidst beds of limestone.

Acton

Because of this stone development began in the 16th century when cottages began to be built by quarrymen employed in the numerous small workings in the area. Most of these quarries have fallen into disuse or have disappeared. However, a small number are still in operation, the nearest being Blacklands Quarry, close to the south edge of the houses. Acton lacks any communal buildings, having no church, shop or pub and many of the cottages are now holiday lets.

Blacklands Quarry

Burngate Stone Carving Centre

Working in stone is widespread all over the Isle of Purbeck.
Just across the road from the access lane to Acton is the Burngate Stone Carving Centre, dedicated to keeping this tradition alive. Within this friendly and modern studio, a group of talented artists and craftspeople offer courses for all ages in stone carving skills, art and rural crafts including, drawing, mosaics, pottery, print making and needlework.
It has a small tea room serving snacks, especially Dorset Apple Cake, gifts made by local and visiting craftspeople and the most amazing views. It is a 'must see' attraction for visitors.

Mount Misery

With quarrying at its peak, the ridge north of Acton down to Wilkswood Farm was a mass of small workings. Littered with piles of grey stone, hovels, sheds, winches and carts, it became known as 'Mount Misery'. In this day and age, only a few quarries survive and the majority of fields are green again.

Where quarrymen once toiled, the landscape is now covered with meadow flowers and flocks of sheep. Banks and hollows, together with the remains of quarr huts, walls, worked stones and a windlass bear witness that this was once a place of industry which has reverted to its original name 'Castle View'.

Overgrown Quarry Pit

Quarr Stones

Norman's Quarry
at
Castle View

Worth Matravers

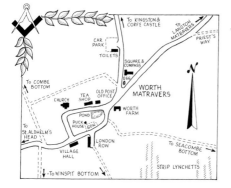

Three miles south of Corfe Castle, Worth Matravers is one of the oldest and prettiest villages on Purbeck and extremely popular with visitors.

The cottages sit comfortably above the Winspit and Seacombe valleys which open on to the coast where the quarries provided the main source of employment for the villagers.

It has a tiny duck pond, beautiful church and a unique pub.

Built over a freshwater spring, the pond has resident Aylesbury ducks which live in a quaint duck house on the green. Close by is a willow tree and a garden which is dedicated to the memory of Percy Wallace, BEM, villager, fisherman and coastguard.

Village Pond and the Duck House

Just across the road by the pond is the old Post Office. Sadly it became a victim to national cutbacks and was closed. It is now a private dwelling.

London Row

Old Post Office

Worth has always maintained strong links with London to which most of its quarried stone was sent to be used in the great buildings of the city. Below the village green, a line of cottages is called 'London Row' to commemorate the partnership. At the foot of the row, a gateway leads onto the path through a valley named 'Winspit Bottom' to the quarry caves. The only building in the valley, a cottage, was the home, for nearly eighty years, of Worth's most celebrated quarryman, William Jeremiah Bower. Always known as 'Billy Winspit', he was a fine fiddle player. Having died in 1966, he was buried in the churchyard where his gravestone bears both his names.

Winspit Cottage

Because of his reputation for secret gift-giving, especially to children, St Nicholas is thought to be the model for the modern Santa-Claus. The 11th century church at Worth is dedicated to St Nicholas of Myra and is one of the oldest religious buildings in Dorset. An almost perfect example of a typical Norman church, its history goes back further than the Conquest, a fact suggested by a blocked up Saxon doorway set in its walls. Comprising a Chancel, Nave and west Tower, only the roof is of comparatively modern construction.

The Church of Saint Nicholas

In the porch is mounted a Celtic cross found in a grave set amidst the remains of an Anchoress's Cell near St Aldhelm's Head. It is thought to date from about 1250 AD.

Corbel Table

Celtic Cross

The main part of the building retains much work carried out in the 12th century and includes a finely carved corbel table of beasts' heads and grotesques.

Graves of Benjamin and Elizabeth Jesty

Close to the north door of the church are the headstones of Benjamin Jesty, pioneer of small-pox inoculation, and of his wife Elizabeth. Jesty, a farmer, came from Yetminster and supported the belief that cowherds and milk-maids who had contracted the mild illness of cow-pox, seemed to be immune to the small-pox virus, a disease which was responsible for the deaths of one third of the population in the 18th century.

With this in mind, in 1774, Jesty inoculated himself, his wife and sons with cow-pox, using a darning needle, thus becoming the first man to carry out the procedure 22 years before Edward Jenner claimed that reputation.

Locally, it was considered a privilege to be treated by Jesty, borne out by Mary Brown's memorial tablet in the church. It notes, with pride, that her mother, Abigail, was personally inoculated by Benjamin Jesty of Downshay. That the treatment appeared to have worked was confirmed by Jesty living to the ripe old age of 79, whilst his wife survived to 84 years old.

The north doorway of the church opens onto the cemetery and is reputed to have been built by the painter, writer and designer Paul Nash in 1934 when he was living in Dorset.

North Door

Village Hall

Down the road from the church gate is the village hall and community centre.
Above the door, an empty belfry suggests that it once served as a schoolhouse.

The Priest's Way

Until 1506, the churchmen of St Nicholas also had responsibility for the chapel in Swanage, regularly making the journey to serve its inhabitants. The route they used can still be walked today via the stone-walled 'Priest's Way' running east along the prehistoric ridgeway path.

The Square and Compass
WORTH MATRAVERS

With the village being the home to generations of quarrymen, it seems fitting that the pub is named after the basic tools of the stonemasons trade.

This fascinating 17th century hostelry must be one of the most unique in the county. Having had little alteration since it was built, it has been run by the Newman family for several generations. During the centuries the pub also served as a meeting place for gangs of smugglers - a trade which involved many a local fisherman and quarry worker. One story tells of a smuggler who, having been shot during a fight with Revenue Officers, was carried to the Square and Compass where he died of his wounds.

Nowadays, most of the custom is from visitors, especially walkers, who take their ease outside on wooden or stone benches. These stand in a garden full of stone carvings and old farm implements amongst which the pub chickens and dogs wander at will.

With magnificent views down the Winspit valley and across the village, it makes the perfect place to be on a sunny afternoon.

Throughout the year, the Square and Compass resonates with live music and dance teams and hosts several festivals, celebrating real ale, cider, pumpkins, stone carving, art and crafts.

The Tap-room

On entering the white painted inn, through a narrow passage, you find yourself faced with a stable-door, the top half of which serves as the bar. To the right is a wood panelled lounge with a welcoming open fire, stone flagged floor and sturdy timber furniture. The tap-room, to the left has a large, open fireplace housing a wood-burner above which, on the mantle, stands a fine collection of old bottles. Both rooms are cluttered with photographs and other relics which give a rare insight into the history of the village, including a smoke stained portrait of Billy Winspit. A frequent visitor to the pub was artist Augustus John and Charles Rennie Mackintosh painted views from the garden. Beyond the tap-room is a tiny museum with exhibits of fossils and items salvaged from wrecks which lie off this dangerous coast. On the corner, below the garden is a beautiful 'stone-egg'. Built by Purbeck Dry Stone Walling, it represents the quarrying industry, whilst the surrounding heavy rope symbolizes the fishermen and a rusty ploughshare on the wall stands for the farmers, all three occupations of the village.

The Drystone Egg

To the north-west of Worth, the plateau is cut by a steep-sided glen which passes by Swanworth quarry and continues down to the sea at Chapmans Pool. Half way along its length, in a small valley, is the 'hidden' hamlet of Hill Bottom. The dwellings were once the homes of fishermen and coastguards. The cottages that remain have been modernised to make for an isolated but unremarkable community.

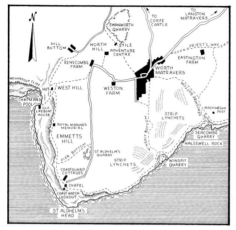

Hill Bottom

Although Renscombe Farm is mainly 17th century, it is built round the remains of a Saxon building which was occupied by monks.
Originally called 'Romescumbe', meaning 'rams valley', it was listed in Domesday Book as a religious cell belonging to Cerne Abbey and possessed 2 cows and 250 wethers. This early period has given rise to a mystery which surrounds the farm.

Renscombe Farm

During the early part of the 20th century, the occupier at Renscombe decided to cut a window in the thick Saxon wall on the west side. As the stones were removed, the wall was found to be hollow and contained a black-clad body of a golden haired girl. Sadly, the corpse disintigrated on contact with the air. Who she was, and what had occurred to warrant such a terrible death at the hands of the monks - we shall never know.

Stone Stile

Astride the path from Hill Bottom up across North Hill is an unusual stile built of quarried stone. It is the only one of this type I have seen.

A further puzzle stands near the highest point of the track below the side of West Hill. A small rendered hut with a large chimney merited a drawing, but I have not discovered its origins or use.

Chapman's Pool

The valley opens to the sea between the unstable grey mud around Chapman's Pool. Once known as Shipman's Pool, this lovely bay, beneath the sheltering cliffs of Houns-tout is a popular anchorage with visiting yachtsmen. A stream runs out of the valley across flat, grey slabs to enter the sea.

These ledges occur throughout the cove, stretching across sand and shingle to disappear under the water, and are best seen at low tide. Chapman's Pool has always been a favourite place for smugglers to land their illegal cargoes. On the south side of the bay is a part natural jetty and a slipway backed by an untidy jumble of boats and fishermen's shacks. At the head of the ramp is a building which once served as a Lifeboat Station. It was built in 1867, possibly as a result of the wreck of a French barque, the 'Georgiana', which was driven ashore and broken up by the sea in 1866. Unfortunately, manning the lifeboat in an emergency was difficult as most of the crew lived some distance away and the station was closed in the 1880s. Surrounded by lobster pots, dinghies, plastic boxes and a rusty anchor, it is now used as a fishing hut.

Slipway and old Lifeboat Station

On the path which runs along the top of Emmett's Cliff, above Chapman's Pool, is a small, but beautiful walled garden which encloses a memorial to those Royal Marines who have lost their lives in action since 1945. Erected by the Royal Marines Association, the walls contain a rockery with stone benches and a picnic table. It is the perfect location for a shrine to Britain's sea soldiers whose motto is :-
'Per mare per terram' - 'By sea by land'.

Royal Marines Memorial

Towering 350 feet above a notorious tide-race, St Aldhelm's Head is one of the most impressive and interesting sites on the Jurassic Coast of Dorset. Its vertical cliffs and steep scree slopes mark the edge of the limestone plateau which stretches south-west of Worth. For many centuries its highest point has been used as a lookout post, known in local dialect as a 'tout' and is the southernmost point of the Isle of Purbeck. Capped with an

Saint Aldhelm's Head

ancient and unusual chapel, it is a favourite spot with visitors and walkers.

Pier Bottom

Between Emmett's Hill and St Aldhelm's Head the path drops steeply into Pier Bottom. This grassy and rabbit-ridden combe no longer boasts the jetty which once stood at its foot. In 1838, two French ships, a brig and a chasse-marie, were wrecked just off the pier. The gentle incline rises to the spoil heaps of St Aldhelm's Quarry.

A mixture of old and new, this jagged hole is the only working stone quarry on the coastline around Worth.   Modern cranes, drills and cutting tools sit amongst old quarr huts and the timbers of an original derrick. It is the only survivor of this type of hand-winched crane left on Purbeck.

The quarry is an important source of 'spangle', a stone which sparkles due to its content of calcite crystals.

St Aldhelm's Quarry

The chapel on St Aldhelm's Head is distinctly Norman in architecture, thought to have been built around 1170 AD. Its heavily buttressed walls support a pyramid shaped roof topped by a 19th century cross on a circular cresset. In the dark interior, a huge central pier supports a vaulted roof, with the only source of light coming from a small lancet window set above the altar.

The central pillar is covered in carved inscriptions, some dating from the 17th century. Through the years, the chapel has also been used as a defensive blockhouse and by Revenue Officers on the lookout for smugglers. A 16th century print shows a beacon tower nearby.

St Aldhelm's Chapel

Coastguard Cottages

A stone's throw from the chapel stands a prominent terrace of neat white cottages.

Built in 1854, they originally housed the families of the coastguards who kept watch from the tout.

Due to cut-backs, the permanent coastguards have disappeared and the dwellings are now private homes.

Coast-Watch Post

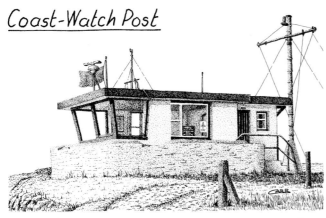

The importance of St Aldhelm's as Purbeck's main lookout point and its role concerning not only the safety of seafarers but also the defence of the realm is borne out by further evidence to be seen on the head.

On top of the point is a modern observation post manned by volunteers of the Coast Watch Service.

A few yards to the east of this glass fronted eyrie, a memorial commemorating a different type of lookout stands on the

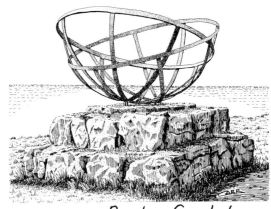

Radar Sculpture

cliff edge. A semi-circular framework of shiny, metal laths on a quarried plinth recalls the work of the experimental Radar Research Establishment which stood in fields, half a mile to the north of the monument during World War II.

On the edge of a quarried ledge, below the lookout post is a 'T' shaped column of stone left by quarrymen possibly as a 'sea-mark'.

A set of concrete steps leads down to an overgrown, ruined building. This housed staff of RAF Worth Matravers working on the radar equipment. Originally, the building may have served the old quarry.

RAF Ruins

Sea Mark

Winspit Quarry

Below Worth the path down Winspit Bottom passes between East and West Man, the slopes of which are lined with fine examples of medieval stripfields known as 'Lynchets'. Dotted with hundreds of mole hills ('oont hills' in local dialect) the terraces are best viewed in late afternoon on a sunny day when shadows are cast.

Lynchets on West Man

The quarry is made up of carved ledges backed by sheer cliffs which are honeycombed with massive quarried caves and galleries. The western terrace is bordered by large, overgrown spoil heaps which enclose the ruins of old buildings. The ledge is open to the south where once, stone was winched down the cliffs to waiting barges.

The main terrace at Winspit

Inside the galleries, huge columns of stone give the impression of an old underground civilisation. However, the only occupants are the ever declining numbers of Mouse-Eared and Greater Horseshoe bats.

Despite the hazard of roof collapses, the Winspit caves are open for public access.

Seacombe Quarry

This was the largest coastal quarry on Purbeck and was in operation from 1700 until 1930.   During the very early years of World War II, many of its spoil heaps were removed to be turned into hardcore for military aerodromes in the New Forest. Its deep, cavernous galleries are now reserved for colonies of bats and public access is prohibited.

They are now in a dangerous condition with rock falls and collapses often occurring. The quarry is noted for its wide, flat ledges where once, barges were loaded and have now become a popular spot for bathers during the summer months.

On the hillside to the east, overlooking the quarry is another wartime relic. The rusting dome of a machine gun post lies half hidden in long grass. Put there in 1940, the gunner must have found this metal cocoon a bitterly cold post in the winter.

Halsewell Rocks

Gun Post

Of all the shipwrecks which have occurred off Purbeck, none made such a mark on local history as that of the 'Halsewell' which foundered on rocks just to the west of Seacombe on the night of 6th January 1786. As the ship broke up, 180 of the 242 souls on board managed to scramble ashore where some found shelter in a cave whilst others clung precariously to the rocks. With 200 feet of sheer cliff above them, and in a howling gale, there seemed no hope of rescue.

Come dawn however, two brave crew members managed to scale the cliffs and stagger to the nearest dwelling, Eastington Farm. The owner, a Mr Garland, organised a rescue team with ropes and managed to save 74 people.

Seacombe Bottom

168 souls lost their lives in the tragedy and those bodies recovered were buried in the level part of Seacombe Bottom.

Eastington Farm

Kingston & the Golden Bowl

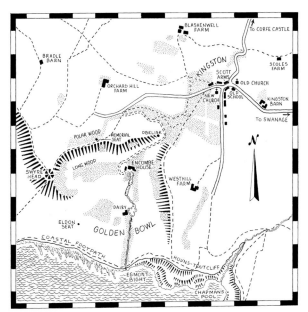

The village of Kingston stands on a ridge one mile to the south of Corfe Castle and is visible for miles around, mainly due to the huge tower of one of its two churches. It commands by far, the finest view of Corfe Gap and the castle.

Although the village has existed since Saxon times – King Ethelred was crowned there, it is, in reality an Estate village, almost completely rebuilt in the 1780s and '90s. The benefactor was William Morton Pitt of nearby Encombe House. Having inherited a vast fortune from his father John, he used the money to improve the living standards of the villagers.

As well as housing and an inn, he also provided a reading room, poorhouse and a factory making rope and sailcloth. The latter came about because he was aware of local men involved in poaching and smuggling. The factory on South Street was an attempt to give them gainful employment and woo them away from their illicit pursuits.

Main Street Kingston

The Scott Arms

The only hostelry in Kingston, it was originally called the 'New Inn', then became the 'Eldon Arms' and finally its present name. It has a lovely garden with amazing views.

Village Pump

A lovely gate leads to a private dwelling with a chapel annexe. The building was originally the village schoolhouse.

This fine example of an old, stone water pump stands outside of the Post Office set at the end of a terrace of cottages.

Old Schoolhouse

The Churches of St James

In 1807, Encombe and Kingston were acquired by John Scott, 1st Earl of Eldon and Lord Chancellor of England. It was he who built the original Gothic style Church of St James in 1833. Erected on the site of an earlier chapel, it stands on a rise to the east of the village. After being 'put out of business' by the 'new' church in 1880, it was utilised as a church hall, then left to decay. Now in private hands, it sits rather forlornly amidst encroaching foliage and an array of dilapidated vehicles.

The Old Church

It was the 3rd Earl, also named John Scott who had the new church built in the 1870s, providing work to local masons for seven years. The building of this 'miniature cathedral' included a large, rounded apse, a conical roof, pointed turret and a huge tower which dominates the village.
Its peal of eight bells is a big attraction for campanologists and visitors alike.
George Street, the architect employed on the church, said of it:-
"It is a pleasure to be allowed to make work so much after one's own heart as this will be. I think it is quite the jolliest church I have built."

The New Church

From the Scott Arms, the road runs down hill towards Corfe Castle. Approximately half a mile below Kingston, off a sharp bend, a lane leads off to the right. It terminates at a gate of the oldest inhabited house in the area, Scoles Farm, now named as a manor.

The building is a fine example of 17th century architecture and is constructed around a small medieval hall-house with a chapel, and was the

Scoles Manor

holding of William de Scoville.   One of the 13th century western walls contains a set of 'Bee-boles' which are recessed to protect the straw 'Bee-skeps' from the weather. These were used throughout the country before the advent of the modern bee hive and were often raided by local mead brewers for the honey.

Reputed to be haunted, the house and converted barns cater for guests. With a lovely landscaped garden, it is well worth exploring.

Bee-boles in the Medieval Wall

Bee-Skep

Blashenwell Farm

Beyond the last cottage at the top of Kingston, a track drops through woods to Blashenwell Farm. The buildings are mainly 18th century but stand in an area which has been shown to be the oldest occupied site on Purbeck. The reason for settlement was the spring which emerges to the south of the farm buildings. Its water contained calcium carbonate which, over the millennia, created a 20 acre, white tufaceous deposit which has preserved the debris of the evolving inhabitants. Archeological study of bones and flint tools have shown the site to have been lived on since around 5,300 BC. During the Iron Age, Roman and medieval periods the area was heavily quarried.

The water properties gave rise to the name of the farm, 'Blachenwelle' meaning 'spring where cloth is bleached.'

Iron Waterwheel

By the 19th century, the spring had been enclosed in a reservoir. From this, water was fed to drive the large, iron waterwheel situated by the main barn, where it powered machinery. The water then flowed out to create the pond which fronts the house, and then into a stream to flow down towards Corfe Castle.

The site is of such importance that it is still being studied by archeologists.

The Golden Bowl and Encombe House

Encombe House is a beautiful property consisting of a long, low building with lawns and lakes set in a sheltered valley known as the 'Golden Bowl'. Enclosed by a crescent of hills, the estate contains its own farm and dairy together with two man-made lakes. The valley must have provided good grazing for thousands of years for, during the 19th century, the fossils of elephant, rhinoceros and reindeer were found on West Hill.

The Golden Bowl

Encombe House

Encombe and Kingston were once two separate manors owned by Shaftesbury Abbey.   In 1604, William Pitt bought Kingston and his descendant, George Pitt purchased Encombe for his son John in 1734, thus amalgamating the two estates.

Encombe is now a private home, having recently been sold for 20 million pounds.

To the north east of the house stands a 40 ft. high obelisk of Purbeck stone. It was erected by Lord Eldon in honour of his elder brother Sir William Scott, Lord Stowell.

Arms of John Scott 1st Earl of Eldon

Encombe Obelisk

The western perimeter of the 'Golden Bowl' is marked by a long ridge culminating on the majestic summit of Swyre Head. At a height of 666 feet, it is the highest point on the Purbeck coast.

The top is capped with a Bronze Age burial mound over 8 feet high Its flat top is crowned with a stone slab offering a seat from which there are fine views of the coast and countryside.

To the south-east of the Head, Eldon Seat sits within the private land of the Encombe Estate. This massive stone block, 8 feet long and 4 feet wide, with a raised backrest was erected in memory of the 1st Earl in 1835 by his daughter, Lady Elizabeth Repton.

Close by the seat, a block of stone marks the grave of 'Pincher', the Lord Chancellor's favourite dog. A German Spaniel, he outlived his master by two years.

A grassy track heads gently north-east from the tumulus

passing between Polar and Long woods. By the wall, a memorial seat commemorates those who died in two plane crashes which occurred nearby in 1938 and 1945.

Kimmeridge

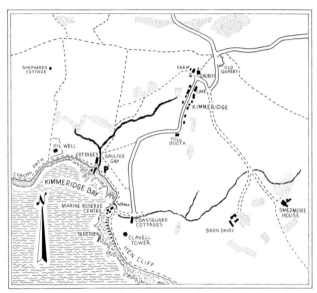

Set on the coast between Tyneham Cap and Smedmore Hill, the village of Kimmeridge is sensibly placed a mile or so from the sea. Sited in a small valley, it consists of a short street which runs south from the church and is lined with attractive thatched cottages.

The name derives from the Old English 'cyme' and 'ric' meaning 'a convenient track'.

Until 1539, the manor was owned by Cerne Abbey, after which it was acquired by Sir William Uvedale who sold it to the Clavells of Smedmore in 1554.

The village is made up of the small church, a farm, cottages and houses, some dating from the 17th century, a community hall, restaurant and some of the loveliest gardens to be found on Purbeck. The latter can be visited by the public once a year when an open day is held. One garden has a fine collection of fossils, but these are to be moved to a museum planned for the village.

There used to be a hostelry in Kimmeridge called the 'New Inn' which has long since closed. However, its building now houses the excellent Clavell's Restaurant and the village shop. It is run by a local farming family and is a boon to the community, visitors and walkers.

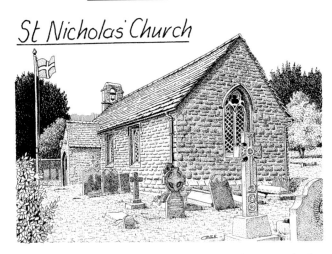

Clavell's Restaurant

St Nicholas' Church

This tiny church is Norman in origin, having been built during the 12th century. At only 56 feet long and 15 feet wide, it consisted of just a nave and chancel. A porch was added a hundred years later and a bell-cote in the 1400s. Rebuilding in Victorian times included a vestry added on to the west wall. It was one of 16 Dorset churches without a dedication until St Nicholas was chosen in the late 20th century.

Just inside the entrance stands the bowl of the original 12th century font on a modern plinth. During Victoria's reign, this had been removed and replaced by one which was described as:-
"extremely and utterly unsuitable for its purpose".
Fate stepped in during the 1920s when workmen, digging in the village found the medieval font in a ditch. It was returned to the church, whilst the 19th century eyesore is believed to have been utilised as a bird-bath.

Medieval Font

Beyond the church porch, against the wall, stands a row of six gravestones. They commemorate Coastguards from Kimmeridge who met their end in a series of tragedies from drowning to shooting.

The inscriptions are virtually illegible but plans are to have them restored.

By the eastern entrance gate there is a group of memorials to members of the Clavell-Mansel family, many of whom served in the Rifle Brigade.

Coastguard Graves

Toll-Booth

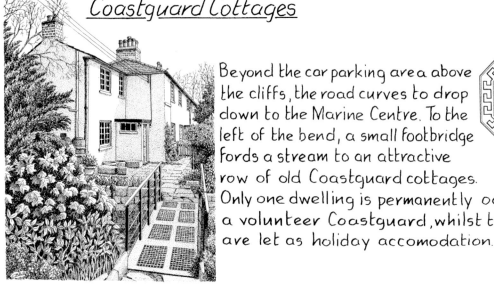

A short distance from the village, the road to the sea takes a sharp right-hand turn. On the bend is a hut acting as a toll-booth where motorists are required to pay a fee before driving down to the bay.

Coastguard Cottages

Beyond the car parking area above the cliffs, the road curves to drop down to the Marine Centre. To the left of the bend, a small footbridge fords a stream to an attractive row of old Coastguard cottages.

Only one dwelling is permanently occupied by a volunteer Coastguard, whilst the remainder are let as holiday accomodation.

South east of Kimmeridge is the elegant Smedmore House, home of the Clavell-Mansel family. Built originally in medieval times, the house now has a Georgian facade added in the 1760s. The Clavells acquired Smedmore during the Tudor period and, for six centuries it has passed by inheritance and marriage to the Clavell-Mansels of today. The family history is not

Smedmore House

equalled anywhere in Dorset, for their line can be traced back to Walter de Claville, a Norman knight who came to England with William the Conqueror and held the manor of Church Knowle, only two miles from Smedmore.

Clavell Tower stood on the highest point of Hen Cliff above Kimmeridge Bay for nearly two centuries. It was built as a folly by Rev. John Richards after 1817 when he inherited the Clavell estate and, as a nephew, adopted the family name. After his death in 1833, the tower was used as a lookout post, with several cannons placed around it. By the 20th century, it had fallen into ruin and, due to cliff erosion, was in danger of collapsing into the sea. In 2007, the Landmark Trust undertook the enormous task of moving the whole tower 25 feet inland and refurbishing it as a de-luxe holiday home. Sadly, it has lost the romantic and mysterious air it had as a ruin.

Old Tower

New Tower

Kimmeridge Bay

Once known as Botteridge Pool, the bay at Kimmeridge is unique on the Dorset coastline, both in its appearance and fascinating history. With a pebble beach, cliffs of black, bitumous oil shale and long, grey ledges, it is not an ideal spot for bathing. There is a strange atmosphere about the whole place, and one can understand why it was once called the 'haunted bay'. With its high oil content, the shale was once used as a foul smelling solid fuel and was known as 'poor people's coal'. The richest and hardest shale is called 'blackstone' and can be worked and polished into jet-like objects. Examples of this art date from 400 BC when it was used to carve ornaments and bracelets. The Romans made luxury items by turning and carving then buffing it to a high gloss using beeswax. Thousands of small shale discs, often found, were a puzzle for many years. At one time it was thought to have been used as currency. This 'coal money' is actually waste cores from lathe-turned objects. An unearthed skeleton was found to have been buried with a large pot of these 'Kimmeridge Pennies', perhaps he was a shale worker. Close to the slipway by the Marine Centre, the stream cascades over the cliff - it has been known to freeze in winter.

The Waterfall

Export Point

Below Hen Cliff, Export Point was a stone-pier built in 1860 by the Wanostacht Company of Wareham. Now in ruins, it was used to load shale onto boats for despatch to their works at Calstock in Cornwall where gas and oil were extracted from the ore. The gas they produced was used to light the streets of Paris.

Marine Centre

Below Clavell Tower is a slipway with wooden boat houses and a cluster of fishermen's huts. In some of these buildings, the Fine Foundation Marine Centre has been established. Manned by volunteers of the Dorset Wildlife Trust, its aim is to inform and educate visitors in caring for the diverse marine environment to be found in the bay.

Inside the Information Centre is a collection of objects found on the shoreline and examples of dinosaur bones and fossils. Eight fish tanks contain living displays of native fish, corals, crabs and sea anenomies. There is also a live seabed camera showing underwater views.

At Gaulter Gap, half way along the bay, a stream runs below a row of what were shale workers cottages. It enters the sea by an old pill-box and 'dragon's teeth' tank traps, relics of World War II.

Gaulter Gap

The treacherous shale ledges stretch out to sea for up to 2 miles and have resulted in many a shipwreck, though only 300 metres of them are visible at low tide. Covered with red and green seaweed, they are pitted with rock pools rich with shells, fish and tiny crustaceans.

Kimmeridge Ledges

During the 17th century, Sir William Clavell made several attempts to create industries in the bay, based on its shale. Using it as fuel, he tried producing salt from seawater, also starting a glass making business. His biggest venture was a proposal to extract Alum from the blackstone. He also built a tramway along Hen Cliff to transport rock to his 'harbour', now recorded as Clavell's Hard on the O.S. map. All these ventures failed, as did that of a French company who used the shale to make varnish, naptha, pitch and oil. The process, carried out at their factory in Weymouth, was so noxious that it was closed down on health and safety grounds.

The 'Nodding Donkey'

It was not until 1959 that the real wealth of Kimmeridge was discovered. B.P. drilled to a depth of 1816 feet and found oil just west of Gaulter Gap. A small 'Nodding Donkey' pump monotonously drew oil to the surface, and continues to do so to this day. This was the forerunner to the start of the Dorset oil boom for, in 1974, the 'black gold' was found in great quantities 3,000 feet below Wytch Farm near Corfe Castle.

Tyneham - The Ghost Village

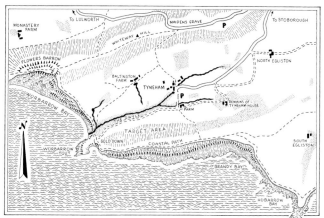

The road which runs south from Stoborough crosses the ridgeway via a hairpin bend where stands a white gate and flagpole. This is the entrance to the MoD live firing ranges and, if there is no red flag flying, entrance is permitted. Carry straight on and after a few hundred yards, a fork to the left is signposted to Tyneham. This allows descent into a landscape which, despite the military activities is, in natural history terms, the most unspoilt valley in Dorset. The road terminates in the car park of the deserted 'ghost' village of Tyneham. A collection of shell-torn cottages and the scattered ruins of farms stand in the shade of ever-encroaching trees, only the church and school remain intact. The manor house has gone, as have the people who once cultivated this lovely place.

The reason for this devastation was World War II, but does not lie with enemy action.

In November 1943, the War Department requisitioned the land and evicted the entire population of the valley in order to use it as part of the artillery and tank firing ranges. Despite promises to return the property to its rightful owners after the war, the military still occupy the area and not a soul has been allowed back into their homes.

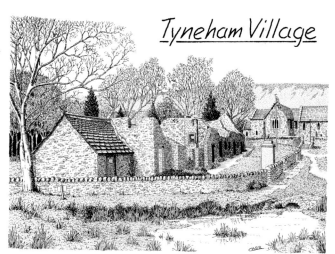

Tyneham Village

It was not always like this, for the land was farmed as far back as the Bronze Age and the four settlements of Baltington, Tyneham, North and South Egliston were all recorded in Domesday Book. The manor of Tyneham was first held by Robert de Mortain, half brother to William the Conqueror, and he built the original house. In the 14th century, the owners were the Russells who added a timber-trussed hall as a south-west wing to the manor. By 1532, the estate had been bought by John Williams of Herringston, passing finally, through marriage to the Bond family who retained it until 1952. The building then suffered much under the military and, when its state became too dangerous, it was demolished by the army.

1928 Phone Box

Post Office Row

The cottage ruins of Post Office Row contain details of each family who dwelt there. The southernmost building was occupied by a shepherd whilst, next door, the Post Office still retains the surprisingly, undamaged telephone box.

The pond was used as a livestock watering place and was a great spot to catch young eels for use as bait. One fisherman was reputed to have stored the elvers in his hat, then wearing it until the time came to use them.

The undamaged church of St Mary stands in isolation on a mound above Post Office Row. Cruciform in plan, the original church was built in the 13th century and the whole building repaired in 1744. It has no tower, but there is a bell-cote in which were hung two bells. One is now stored in Steeple church and the other hangs at West Parley in Bournemouth.

Church of St Mary the Virgin

Open to the public, the church is also a museum which houses a huge amount of information about the history of the people of Tyneham, including a series of coloured tiles in the nave and transepts displaying the family names.

Water Tap and Trough

Set into the churchyard wall is an elaborate water tap and trough. The inscription, dated 1853, reads:-

> Whosoever drinketh of this water shall thirst again; but whosoever shall drink of the water that I shall give him shall never thirst; but the water that I shall give him shall be in him a well of water springing into everlasting life

The Old Schoolhouse

A few yards along the road, opposite the church, is the old schoolhouse. Though it actually closed in 1932, eleven years before the evictions, it has been beautifully restored to the condition it was in when still in use.

In the church, an exhibit of the school diary bears the poignant entry by a teacher :-

"Closed the school today."

The school is open to the public.

The inside of the building has been re-created in such a way to give the impression that the children have just gone out into the playground.

Rows of desks with exercise books, a blackboard, piano and teaching aids provide a nostalgic insight into our educational past. In the entrance lobby, a row of coat pegs is labelled with the name of each pupil.

Schoolroom

Tyneham Farm

At the far end of the car park a bridge leads to Tyneham Farm, a big attraction for visitors, not least for the toilet block by the entrance.

Excellent work on restoring this site began in 2009 and carried out by the Dorset Conservation Volunteers. Sadly, the farmhouse itself was beyond salvage, but the outbuildings were not. The Great Barn, granary, stables, cowsheds and pond now provide a wonderful insight into farming as it used to be. Scattered throughout is a fine collection of farming implements and artifacts. To the right of the entrance, rustic shelving supports an interesting display of agricultural implements and an array of spent ammunition salvaged from the surrounding firing ranges.

Stable Block

Milk Churns and Creamer

Spent Artillery Shells

<u>Haywain</u>

The Great Barn has been adapted as an instructional area for schoolchildren and visiting groups. A small theatre, originally installed by the Bond family, occupies most of the building and now has a new lease of life. A haywain, beautifully restored, takes up the opposite end against a background of farming tools.

From the farm, a well surfaced track leads to Worbarrow Bay almost a mile away. It follows the route of the 'Gwyle', a Dorset dialect name for a steep-sided, heavily wooded glen with a stream. The Gwyle at Tyneham is the finest example of its kind on Purbeck, others being found at Encombe, Rempstone and Church Knowle.

<u>The head of the Gwyle</u>

The slopes of Gold Down, to the left of the track are littered with the misshapen hulks which the visitor cannot help but notice.
These are the battered remains of armoured vehicles used as live-firing targets by tanks based at Lulworth.

Worbarrow Bay

At the mouth of the Gwyle is the long, pebble beach of Worbarrow Bay, which curves away to Mupe Rocks. The cliffs are of multi-coloured Wealdon Sand which rises to the chalk of Flowers Barrow. The track ends amidst ruins and foundations of old cottages, witness to the bay supporting a thriving community until the wartime evictions.
Traces of an Iron Age settlement show that it was occupied in much older times.

At the eastern end, jutting out into the sea, is the 180 feet high, conical shape of Worbarrow Tout. Capped with grass, this limestone mass marks the western limit of the beds of Purbeck marble.
At its foot is a flat area which, in Victorian times, supported a long range of Coastguard buildings, its officers keeping watch from the summit of the tout.

Worbarrow Tout

The Ridgeway and Ghostly Tales

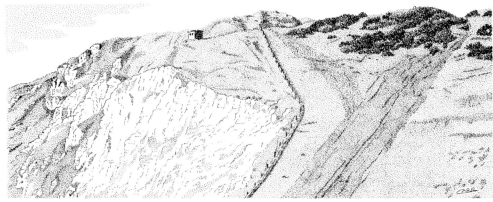

Southern path to Flowers Barrow

From Worbarrow Bay, the Coastal Path climbs steeply northwards past a W.W.II pill-box to the irregular heights of Flowers Barrow. This Iron-Age hill fort stands at the seaward end of the ridgeway and marks the western boundary of the Isle of Purbeck. In ancient times, this ditched and banked fortress must have been impressive but coastal erosion has caused the southern defences to

Inside the fort

collapse into the sea. Captured by the 2nd Legion Augusta during the Roman Conquest, the summit provides a wonderful viewpoint over the little cove of Arish Mell and the Mupe Rock ledges. From Flowers Barrow, a stile leads you onto the ridgeway path, passing eastwards above Tyneham and traversing Whiteway and Povington Hills to the slopes above Creech.

On the lower, southern slopes of Whiteway Hill are the ruins of Baltington Farm. Set amongst traces of Celtic fields and an ancient settlement, Baltington was already old when William the Conqueror compiled the Domesday Book. With its dark pond, encroaching vegetation and the mournful cawing of rooks, the farm has a brooding atmosphere, only heightened by the tale of suicide attached to it. The ruin stands

Baltington Farm

within the live-firing danger area and access requires permission from the military.

Atop the ridgeway, in the area where the tarmac road bends sharply, lies the source of a ghostly legend. During the 18th century, a young milkmaid, Jane Gilbert, working at Baltington Farm, on being spurned by her lover, took her own life by hanging herself in a cowshed. As a suicide, she could not be buried within the Parish. Therefore, her body was interred on the boundary close to an ancient cross

tracks on the ridge. To mark the spot, a coffin was carved into the trunk of an oak tree near what came to be known as 'Maiden's Grave Gate', where Jane's spectre is said to appear. Terrible screams are reputed to be heard on the beach where once a smuggler was stoned to death by Revenue men. Across the centuries, dozens of witnesses have reported seeing phantom Roman Legionaries marching in formation along the ridgeway.

It is no wonder that Tyneham has earned the reputation as the 'Ghost Village'.

Creech and Steeple

Creech is not a village in the conventional sense, having no focal point other than Creech Barrow Hill. It consists of a sprawling community made up of cottages and farms dotted around its lower slopes, the hill dividing it into Creech and East Creech.

Its largest building is the beautiful manor house, the Grange, set in what is reputed to be the most perfect landscape in the county.

Built by Sir Oliver Lawrence in the 16th century, the original manor was burnt down by Cromwell's troops during the Civil War.

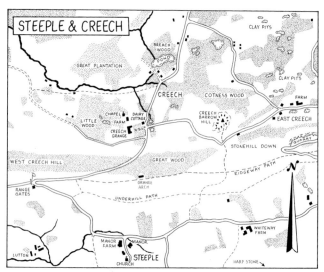

The ruins were bought by Nathaniel Bond in 1691 and his family restored the house over the next 150 years. In 1746, Dennis Bond, the son of Nathaniel, began building the Chapel of St John the Baptist in the grounds. He utilised bits of the derelict Priory at East Holme, including a wonderful 12th century archway. The Bonds lived at Creech until 1979, since when it has been the property of private owners, the latest being Mr Hayward.

Creech Grange

Chapel of St John

The Bond family were also responsible for building London's Bond Street during the reign of Charles II, and unsurprisingly, the road which runs past Creech Grange is called Old Bond Street. Typical of the buildings in Creech, Dairy Cottage stands on the corner of the lane leading to the farm and the estate chapel.

At East Creech, small thatched cottages cluster around the farmhouse with its attractive duck pond. The farm has good camping and caravanning facilities.

Dairy Cottage

The countryside around Creech has always provided income and employment. Amidst the farms, a multitude of ponds and lakes are flooded remains of old clay quarries. The largest of these is Breach Pond, once worked by the Pike Brothers. Like many of the ponds, it is now a haven for anglers.

East Creech Farm

Breach Pond

Gate to the Firing Ranges

From Creech, the road rises steeply to the ridge and the sharp bend by the entrance gates to the firing ranges, previously mentioned in the Tyneham section. There is a large car park to the left, from which a footpath leads to the eastern part of the ridgeway. A short walk brings you to another famous Purbeck folly, 'Grange Arch'. Built by Dennis Bond around 1740, this crenellated structure overlooks the manor house. With a large arch and two stepped bays, topped with pyramids, it was designed as an 'eye-catcher' to be seen from below, a view now hidden by the tall trees.

Grange Arch

Creech Barrow - Purbeck's 'Volcano'

On approaching Creech from Wareham, you cannot help but notice a prominent mound seemingly set apart from the ridge.
This is Creech Barrow Hill which at 634 feet, is one of the highest points on the Island and offers some of the best panoramic views in Dorset. When seen from the west, it appears to have a double summit, the result of a large Bronze Age barrow, giving rise to its nickname of the 'Purbeck Volcano'.

The northern slopes are densely covered in the trees of Cotness Wood within which once operated the Victorian brickworks of Arthur Cobb, a local farmer, all traces of which have now disappeared.

The approach path up the southern slope rises to the first of the two peaks, cutting through the ancient burial mound to the triangulation pillar which marks the summit. Close by is a recently installed, white stone seat, very welcome after the climb. It bears the inscription:-

'Everything has to be earned, but anything is possible'.

The top of the hill is dotted with limestone outcrops, some of which are shaped giving a clue to their origin. They are the remains of a royal hunting lodge of King John, one of three known on Purbeck. It would have been a substantial tower manned by a Warrener. By the 16th century, it had fallen into decay and was demolished, the stones being carried off for use in other building projects.

Church of St Michael - Steeple

Half a mile below the ridgeway almost due south of Grange Arch, the tiny hamlet of Steeple is one of the hidden gems of Purbeck. Consisting of just a manor house, farm, church and rectory, it comes under the jurisdiction of the incumbent squire at Creech Grange. Most visitors who find Steeple do so by accident, mistaking the entrance lane for the nearby road to Kimmeridge. If they do drive in, they immediatly turn back and depart, for this place of peace and tranquility has the appearance of being a private enclosure. A driveway passes the farm and manor house to a tree-lined mound surmounted by the Church of Saint Michael and All Angels. Sheltered by massive yew trees, it belies the name of the hamlet as it has a square tower.

In 1540, the Lawrence family came to Steeple as lords of the manor. An ancestor, Edmund Lawrence, had married Agnes Washington in 1390 and their Coats of Arms, a *'Crusader Cross'* (Lawrence) and *'Bars and Mullets'* (Washington) were heraldically joined. Whilst the Lawrences moved to Dorset, a descendant of the Washingtons settled in Virginia in America where he was destined to become the great-grandfather of George Washington, the first President of the USA. His Arms *'Bars and Mullets'* in modern terms are *'Stars and Stripes'* and are thought to be the origin of the American national flag.

Carvings of these quartered Arms are set in the church porch, above the east door and as scarlet-painted bosses inside the roof of the nave.

This delightful manor house was built during the reign of Queen Elizabeth I and enlarged in the 17th century. A panel on the front of the building, dated 1698 commemorates the remodelling of the manor by Roger and Ruth Clavell.

Steeple Manor

Once the home of the vicar of St Michael's, the Rectory has become a private house and the church now comes under the jurisdiction of the rector at Church Knowle.

The Old Rectory

Harp Stone

Half a mile to the south-east of Steeple, just inside the edge of a small wood is a 7 foot high monolith, the 'Harp Stone'. Its origins are unknown, but it is thought to have served as a waymark on an ancient track between Creech and Kimmeridge.

Church Knowle

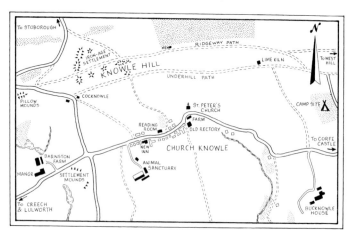

The delightful village of Church Knowle lies just two miles west of Corfe Castle, its buildings clustered around the road which crosses the ridgeway to Creech. Its name derives from the Old English words 'cerise' and 'cnol' meaning 'church on a hilltop', and was recorded in Domesday Book as 'chenolle'. It grew from a series of small, oblong settlements granted by William the Conqueror to his supporters. Church Knowle went to Walter de Claville the founding ancestor of the Clavell Family of Smedmore House.

Though now a quiet place, best known for its inn and animal sanctuary, the village once had a Post Office, Dairy and a Reading Room. To serve the area there also existed a mason, a brickmaker, two cobblers and two blacksmiths.

Although now grown to include some 20th century houses, the village retains many of its old buildings. The prettiest cottage is said to be the 17th century Church Farm which stands opposite the parish church at the entrance to the village.

Church Farm

Church of St. Peter

This charming church retains much of its 13th century origins and the high ground on which it stands is thought to be the remains of a Bronze Age burial mound. The tower, with its pyramid shaped roof was rebuilt in 1741, with further alterations carried out in 1830. Inside, the gallery has a display of historical photographs and there is a memorial to John Clavell dated 1572 in the form of a stone carved, canopied tomb.

It is reputed that, in 1323, a poacher named Robert Hardle, having killed the King's deer and wounded the sub-Constable of Corfe Castle, took sanctuary in the church. He managed to escape 'over the hill', the local term for the far side of the ridgeway. The noted quarry owners, John and William Pike, are buried in the churchyard.

On the corner below St Peter's the Rectory was re-built in Mock-Tudor style by the Rev. Owen Luttrel Mansel in the late 19th century. Now a private house, the annual village Summer-Fête is held within its grounds.

The Old Rectory

The New Inn

The village pub, the New Inn has a good reputation for fine ales and excellent food, especially its fish menu. The building began life as a farm, the main barn, now thatched, becoming the original pub. Its name has been lost in the mists of time and it now serves as a lounge bar.

In later years, the inn expanded to incorporate the farm dairy, the stone-roofed building next door.

Beyond the New Inn there is a row of residential cottages, mainly dating from the 17th century. At the end of this terrace, a quaint, lean-to building was once the village Post Office and Shop, now sadly a victim of modern day closures.

Old Post Office

The Reading Room.

In 1887, Rev. Mansel provided the village with a Reading Room to celebrate the Golden Jubilee of Queen Victoria. Having closed as such by the 1960s, it is now Grade II listed and has been modernised as a drop-in centre and meeting room.

Built by the d'Estoke family around 1280AD, Barnston Manor is the oldest dwelling in Church Knowle. It retains the hall and solar wing of that date and, though additions were made, only essential repairs have been carried out since the 16th century. It has a beautiful frontage with a magnificent Elizabethan bay window. In its land are traces of a medieval field system

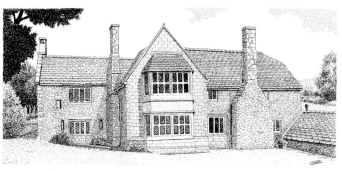

Barnston Manor

and six 'pillow mounds', possibly built as a rabbit warren. Across the road from the main gate, irregular hummocks are all that remains of the original settlement of 'Beorn's Tun'.

Knowle Hill

Behind the manor, the bare whaleback shape of Knowle Hill stretches for over a mile. It can be traversed by either the ridgeway, one of my favourite walks, or by the underhill path, both historically interesting. Near the western end of the ridge are banks and ditches of an Iron-Age settlement.

Approximately half-way along the top of the hill is a memorial erected by the Ramblers' Association. It is dedicated to Mary Baxter, MBE, who worked tirelessly to conserve the Dorset countryside and its footpaths. On the underhill path you will come across the ruins of an old Lime Kiln. Grade II listed, it once supplied Church Knowle with its mortar.

Mary Baxter Memorial

Old Lime Kiln

105

Margaret Green Animal Rescue Centre

Established in 1965, this sanctuary is the oldest animal welfare organisation in Dorset. As a registered charity, it relies solely on donations from visitors, though entry and parking are free.

The Reception Centre is welcoming and full of information, souvenirs, a gift shop and a tea room.

Reception and Shop

Set in picturesque scenery, the centre takes in every kind of animal. The sole aim of the staff and volunteers is to rescue, nurture and hopefully rehouse the creatures in their care. During one visit I was lucky enough to find a farrier busy at work, a rare opportunity to observe an age old craft in action.

The Stables

The Farrier

Corfe Castle Village

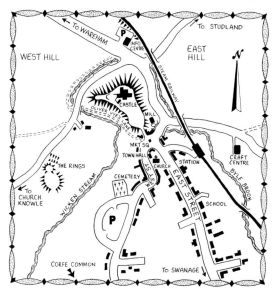

Below the ruins of its famous fortress, Corfe Castle is described as one of the most beautiful villages in Britain, and is known throughout the world.

Its charm and varied past ensure a constant flow of tourists, writers and historians whilst artists and photographers find inspiration wherever they look.

The site of the village has been occupied for thousands of years, a fact borne out by a line of eight Bronze Age burial mounds which are sited on the common, together with traces of Celtic field systems. The footings of a Roman villa were also discovered in the area.

Entrance to the Village

From the 12th century, Corfe built a reputation as the centre of stoneworking on Purbeck, the raw materials being dragged on horse-drawn sleds from the local quarries. The village is built almost entirely of this warm, grey stone, its buildings lining East and West Streets, which meet at the tiny inclined Market Square by the castle entrance.

The Market Square

The view down the Square shows the Bakery and the columned portico of the 'Greyhound Inn', circa 1733.
At the bottom, on East Street, the 'Bankes Arms Hotel' was originally built as a private house in the 1920s but later converted into a hostelry.

Opposite the Bakery is the Town House, once used as a setting in the film of Thomas Hardy's 'The Mayor of Casterbridge'. The room behind the large bay window was, in reality, the Mayor's Robing Room.
Erected in 1897, to honour Queen Victoria, the Market Cross stands on an older plinth.
At the top of the Square is the National Trust shop and Information Centre and the beginning of West Street.
Outside the Post Office stands a memorial sign dedicated to King Edward.
Erected by Francis Newberry of the Glasgow School of Art in the 1920s, when he lived in the village.

The inscription reads:-

The Town House and Cross

> EDWARD THE MARTYR KING OF WESSEX TREACHEROUSLY STABBED AT CORVES GATE IN AD 978 BY HIS STEPMOTHER ELFRIDA

On entering West Street from the Square, on the left is what is reputed to be the smallest Town Hall in Britain. Rebuilt in 1774, with stone for the ground floor and brick for the upper, it still serves as a meeting place and also as the museum. Opposite is an alley leading to the Model Village. Set in a garden, the centrepiece depicts the castle as it was before being destroyed by the troops of Oliver Cromwell. West Street, in particular, played an important role in turning Corfe into the 'marble capital' of Purbeck. Here lived many of the quarry owners amidst the workshops and yards of the 'marblers', men who split and shaped the raw stone. The street stands on a foundation of marble chippings left by the industry which, was at one time reported to be 12 feet thick.

'Marblers'
Splitting
Stone

Before the advent of circular and frame saws, blocks of stone were split using 'plugs' and 'feathers'.
This involved chiselling a line of angular shaped holes into which a wedge (the 'plug') between two strips of metal (the 'feathers') were hammered with sledges until the stone split.

Town Hall and St Edward's Church

Set in a terrace of houses and shops in West Street, the Fox Inn is the oldest and smallest pub in Corfe Castle. Although mainly 18th century, parts of the building date from 1568 and it incorporates a 14th century fireplace. The interior is split level and it has a garden with excellent views of the castle. Sadly, it is currently closed.

The Fox Inn

East Street

The main highway through Corfe, East Street, rises round a sharp bend to pass below the Market Square and the church to continue on to Towns End. Mainly residential, the street also contains shops, a hotel, the school, library and a public house.

The largest building on East Street is Morton's House. Built in 1590 by William Dacombe it was shaped as an 'E' in honour of Queen Elizabeth I. It was extended in 1666 using stone from the castle ruins. The manor remained in the family until 1712 when it was sold to John Morton, whose name has endured.
Eventually, through marriage, it passed to the Bond family and, during the

Morton's House

19th century, was divided into three tenements. The house was then converted and still remains a very comfortable hotel and restaurant with a walled garden.

The Castle Inn is a traditional Dorset pub built in the early 1800s.
It was possibly once the haunt of the author Thomas Hardy, for it is mentioned in his tale 'The Hand of Ethelberta'.

The Castle Inn

On his death in 1606, Sir Edmund Uvedale left a piece of land called New Mills for the building of Almshouses for the poor, which were completed in 1611. In the 18th century, several benefactors remodelled it with four ground floor flats and two upper apartments reached by an unusual, exterior flight of stone steps.
Restored in 1977, the property is now named 'Jubilee House'.

The Almshouses

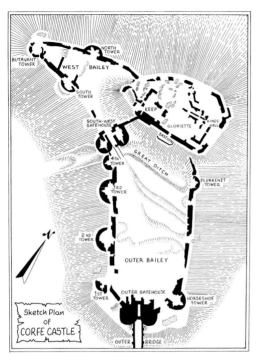

Sketch Plan of CORFE CASTLE

Labels on plan: NORTH TOWER, BUTAVANT TOWER, WEST BAILEY, SOUTH TOWER, SOUTH-WEST GATEHOUSE, KEEP, GLORIETTE, KINGS HALL, BASTION, GREAT DITCH, 4TH TOWER, 3RD TOWER, PLUNKENET TOWER, 2ND TOWER, OUTER BAILEY, 1ST TOWER, OUTER GATEHOUSE, HORSESHOE TOWER, OUTER BRIDGE

Corfe Castle

No matter what delights the village may hold, visitors are drawn to the impressive ruins of the castle looming above the rooftops. Its position is wonderful, on top of a steep hill sitting in a cleft of the Purbeck ridge and protected by the Wicken Stream and Byle Brook which flow around its base to merge into the Corfe River.

No one knows how long this steep hill has been used as a stronghold. Iron-Age man could have built a hillfort, though any indication of this has long disappeared under later building.

Although the Romans knew of it, the Saxons were the first to build anything substantial. We know that, in 978 AD, it had a hunting lodge, possibly with a hall and defensive barricade.

However, it was under the Normans, with their passion for building castles that work began in earnest.

Corfe Castle from West Hill

Wandering within its walls, marvelling at the picturesque ruins and enjoying the panoramic views from the upper levels can be a little misleading, for the history of the castle is bloody!

During Saxon times, when it was but the hunting lodge, the young King Edward was murdered here by his stepmother, Queen Elfrida. She stabbed him by the south-west gatehouse which is now known as the 'Martyr's Gate'.

South West Gatehouse

In 1139, King Stephen laid siege to Corfe, attempting, usuccessfully to defeat one of his rebel barons, Baldwin de Redvers.

To facilitate the blockade, he built a Motte and Bailey castle 400 yards to the south-west. Just banks and ditches remain and are referred to as 'The Rings'.

Castle from 'The Rings'

King John used the castle as his treasury and as a prison, within which he once starved fifteen French knights to death. He also imprisoned Isabel and Margery, daughters of the King of Scotland.

Peter of Pomfret was locked up until John ordered him dragged by a horse to Wareham where he was hung, drawn and quartered.

Edward II was incarcerated at Corfe before being taken to Berkeley Castle where he was brutally murdered by Sir John Mautravers and William Gurney in 1327. It was over 500 years after King Stephen's failed attempt that the defences of the castle were tested again. Two sieges were to give rise to a traitor, a heroine and the downfall of the fortress itself.

Corfe Castle was then occupied by the Bankes family who, at the outbreak of the English Civil War, chose to support the King. In May 1643, while Sir John Bankes was absent, Parliamentary troops attempted to gain entrance to the castle, but John's wife, Lady Mary, had secured the gates. The Roundheads tried to storm the walls, committing 150 Poole seamen equipped with scaling ladders. Mary, together with servants and a few men-at-arms repulsed them by pouring hot ashes onto the attackers as they struggled up the slopes. However, this was the age of gunpowder and artillery, so the besiegers sited a battery of cannons on the old 'rings'. The subsequent bombardment had little effect and Mary held the castle for the following three years.

The Great Keep

Bankes Family Arms

North Tower

114

In 1646 however, a second siege proved successful, due to the actions of a traitor, Thomas Pittman, a Royalist Colonel serving in the castle. He devised a plot to open the gate to admit 'reinforcements' who were in fact enemy soldiers and the small garrison was swiftly overpowered. The Governor, Colonel Anketell, finally surrendered the fortress on the morning of 27th February.

A few days later, Parliament ordered the demolition of Corfe Castle by the use of explosives. This proved almost as ineffective as the artillery bombardment, as the castle would just not blow up. The wonderful masonry resisted destruction, towers refused to collapse, merely leaning at odd angles, or sliding partway down the hill.

I wonder if those engineers imagined that, far from demolishing the fortress, they actually created a future world-wide tourist attraction.

Lady Mary is commemorated by a statue of her in the Bankes family home, Kingston Lacey, near Wimborne. She is depicted holding a sword and the key to the castle she had defended for so long.

Shield of Arms of Alan de Plunkenet, Constable of the castle 1269 - 70. The carving is mounted on the front of the tower he had built during his tenure.

Plunkenet Tower

Main Gate

Entrance to the castle is across a 100 feet long bridge over a deep ditch, which may once have been flooded as a moat. With four arches, it leads to the main gate which is flanked by two large, round fronted towers. Inside the arch, there are

grooves cut into the stone which would have held a portcullis. Beyond the entrance is the open space of the outer bailey, sometimes called the lower ward.

On top of the hill is the inner ward with the Keep and, to its east, an area called the 'gloriette'.

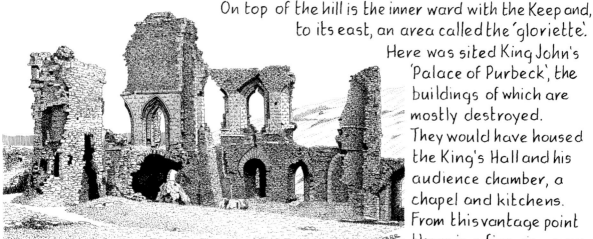

Here was sited King John's 'Palace of Purbeck', the buildings of which are mostly destroyed. They would have housed the King's Hall and his audience chamber, a chapel and kitchens. From this vantage point there is a fine view over the Gap and East Hill.

The Gloriette

Corfe Castle Railway Station

No trip to Corfe Castle is complete without a visit to the Railway Station.
An integral part of the Swanage Steam Railway, it has been beautifully restored by volunteers over many years.
The atmosphere is one of nostalgia, a trip back to the heyday of the train. As well as the buildings, the station incorporates a museum which includes the narrow-gauge steam locomotive 'Secundus' built in 1874.

Once the village milk factory, the Boilerhouse Gallery lies just beyond the station platform at the foot of East Hill.

Boilerhouse Gallery

It is a co-operative gallery specialising in work with a strong Purbeck flavour and produced by local artists. On display there are paintings, pottery, jewellry, sculptures and items made of driftwood. It is a working studio, very welcoming and casual where they don't mind if you are wearing muddy boots.

Boar Mill

At the base of the eastern slope to the castle is Boar Mill and can be seen on entering the village from the Wareham side. The building as it stands is mainly 18th and 19th century but sits on the site of an earlier mill.

In Victorian times it was bought by George Battrick, a baker, and remained a working mill and bakery until the 1950s.

In 1993 it was acquired by the National Trust and access is restricted as it has occupants, a colony of roosting bats.

The castle slopes, just above the mill are said to be haunted by a headless, white lady.

Town's End

A visit to the village of Corfe Castle is well worth a day of anybody's time. The grim ruins of the castle have mellowed over the centuries, mainly due to the care of the National Trust. The chaotic marble workshops of West Street have long disappeared and cottage gardens have blossomed.

Explore the village for yourself, discover its hidden places for there is hardly a corner of Corfe Castle that is not beautiful.

Norden

Just to the north of Corfe Castle, amidst what was once a huge complex of clay mines, is Norden Farm. Though still a working farm, it has diversified into a campsite which can cater for ninety caravans. It has an excellent farm shop dealing in local produce, stock and pet food and gardening supplies. The original Georgian house has been renovated and caters for guests and incorporates a popular restaurant.

Old Grain Store and Shepherds Hut

In contrast to the modern timber-built shop, the farm outbuildings and barns are rather dilapidated, but retain a rustic charm. They contain a jumbled collection of agricultural equipment, tractors and a mobile shepherds hut.

Poultry of all kinds, chickens geese and peacocks wander at will throughout the farm.

A short distance beyond the farm entrance, a roundabout on the main road gives access to Norden Railway Station with its Park and Ride and the Mining Museum. Until 2017 the Swanage Heritage Railway terminated here but the line now extends to Wareham.
Refreshments are available from the 'Nest Buffet'carriage. Built on the former site of a ball-clay works, there is much to see around this tiny station.

Norden Station

On the walkway up to the platform at Norden, the Purbeck Mineral and Mining Museum is fast becoming a popular visitor site. The Island is one of the few places where fine ball-clay can be found and still is a centre for its mining. The museum has taken over a decade to establish and further expansion is planned by the volunteers who have created it.
Buildings and equipment from drift-mine Nº 7 at Norden Farm were donated by Imerys and reconstructed to form the basis of the exhibition. These included the Transhipment Building and the foreman's office, now serving as the Information hut.

Entrance to Mining Museum

In the exhibition hall, there are films, models, equipment and tools used in the industry, and a fine selection of transportation tubs.

Visitors can venture down a simulated mine via a long, dark ramp, at the foot of which is a working face of real clay. The clay was transported to Poole Harbour by a system of narrow-gauge railways which carried tubs across the heathlands.

Transhipment Building and Ramp

Clay working face

At present, volunteers are working to reconstruct some of the track and Engine Shed.

In 2014, the mining museum won the Heritage Railway Association's award for being a:-
'unique, valuable education resource and quality visitor attraction'.

Ideally placed, the museum is well worth going to see and, at the time of writing, entrance is free - though donations are welcome.

Scotland

Scotland Farmhouse

From the roundabout at Norden, a narrow road crosses Middlebere Heath towards
Slepe. A mile up the road, by a sharp left hand bend is Scotland Farm and barn.
Its original construction was the dream of one of the despised 'heathcroppers',
Peter Whefen who, in 1665, decided he would upgrade his status in life.
A poor man, he built his home by utilising stone from the ruins of Corfe Castle
blown up by Cromwell's troops two decades earlier. The result was this sturdy,
low, stone-roofed farmhouse with walls of squared ashlar. It has an attractive
porch with the builders initials carved into the lintel above the entrance.
Almost unchanged since it was built, it is now Grade II listed.

Scotland Barn

Across the yard is an impressive barn with a thatched roof and much bigger than the farmhouse.
In 1982, the property came into ownership of the National Trust who, eight years later, rebuilt the then dilapidated building.

The renovation team was led by master mason Derek Cartridge, who is commemorated by a carved figurehead on the south wall of the barn. On the frontage is set the Trust's logo with the restoration date. The barn now houses a successful business renovating old carts and carriages and employs wheelwrights and a blacksmith.

Derek Cartridge

1990

N.T. Logo

Sharford Bridge

A short distance up the road, public footpaths lead down to Sharford Bridge, situated midway between Scotland and Wytch Farm.

Built around 1700, this packhorse bridge is one of the few clues to an ancient 'lost' road which crossed the heath from Stoborough to the old quay at Ower.

Six feet wide and very overgrown, it is the remotest bridge in Dorset. With twin spans, it crosses the Corfe River, merely a stream at this stage. On the approach to the bridge, embedded in the track, cobblestones can be seen, presumably the remains of the old road

I find Sharford a peaceful place to rest and take in the surrounding countryside. If you are quiet, it is an ideal spot for observing the wildlife, especially birds which flourish around the stream.

The large estate of Rempstone is situated north of Corfe Castle on the far side of the ridgeway. In 1464, the Lord of the manor was Robert Rempstone who had taken his family name from the Old English place name of 'Hring-Stun' meaning 'Stone Ring'. The original part of the hall dates from the 17th century but has been altered and added to ever since. In 1757, it was bought by John Calcraft M.P., one of the richest

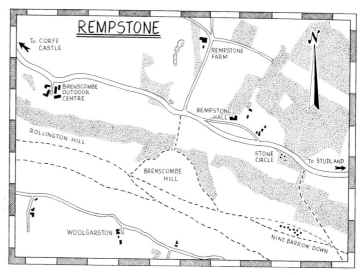

men in England. The house is said to be haunted by the ghost of the religiously fanatical Lady Caroline Calcraft. Her great-great-great grandson, Major Douglas Ryder, known as 'Jack', inherited the estate in 1927, but, during World War II, it was requisitioned by the military. In the 1970s, oil was discovered on Jack's land at Wytch Farm, after which he was nicknamed the 'Sheikh of Dorset'. Jack and his wife, Vee, moved to Bushey House, leaving the estate to be managed by his sons James and Ben. Jack died in 1986 and was buried in an unmarked grave in Rempstone Woods on Nine Barrow Down.

Rempstone Hall

James lived at Rempstone Hall until 2005, after which it came under rental and is managed by his daughter.

By the road, a quarter of a mile to the east of the hall stands an almost hidden gem.

The scattered and damaged remains of a Bronze Age stone circle can be found, almost unseen within a wooded area.

The original circle has been estimated at eighty feet in diameter but many of the stones have been removed or buried.

Rempstone Circle

At one time, an avenue of 26 stones, possibly a processional way, may have led to the circle, but sadly, they were destroyed by a local farmer in 1957.

A short distance down the road to Corfe Castle, in the shadow of Rollington Hill is Brenscombe Farm. Since 1992, it has been developed into Dorset's premier outdoor centre.

With excellent facilities it caters for the education of young people in all aspects of outdoor pursuits from canoeing to rockclimbing and field studies.

Brenscombe Outdoor Centre

Harman's Cross

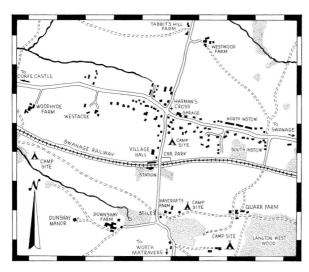

The main road from Corfe Castle to Swanage crosses the most agricultural countryside on Purbeck. Dozens of tiny fields cover the landscape against the backdrop of Nine Barrow Down.

Two miles outside of Corfe, the road passes through Harman's Cross, a residential hamlet mostly built in the 20th century which lacks a significant church or a public house. It does however boast a garage, modern village hall, a manor house and railway station. As the name implies, it stands around a cross roads where Tabbits Hill and Haycrofts Lane meet the main road.

It is reputed that, many years ago, a man named Harman committed such a horrible murder that he was sentenced to be hung and buried in a place far away from decent folk - the cross-roads was the site chosen.

The village itself has little of interest other than the old Woodside Chapel. Originally built by the owner of the garage, it is now a private dwelling.

The surrounding area however, is very popular with visitors, having three good camp sites close by. The village hall is noted for its annual fête, gymkhana and steam and vintage car rally.

Woodside Chapel

Set below the southern edge of the village, the Swanage Steam Railway has the most beautiful, well kept and nostalgic station. With an abundance of flowers and old railway associated items, it is a pleasant place to spend an hour or two. Just to sit on the platform, admiring the scenery and watching the steaming juggernauts of a bygone age, packed with enthusiastic passengers is a great way to relax. The adjacent car park is an excellent starting point for walks through the wonderful surrounding countryside.

Railway Station

Stile leading to Woodhyde Farm

From the railway station, Haycroft Lane rises towards Primrose Hill. At the start of the first bend, a signpost and stile give access to a footpath to Woodhyde Farm and its large campsite.
A few yards up the road from the stile, an almost unnoticed, rough driveway leads to one of Purbeck's hidden treasures, Dunshay Manor.

128

Dunshay Manor

In the early 13th century, Dunshay was a quarrying estate owned by a lady called Alice Breuer who lived in the medieval manor house. She is remembered in history for, in 1220, she made a free gift of quarried marble for the building of Salisbury Cathedral. On the site of her home, the basis of the present manor was built by John Dolling during the middle of the 17th century.

In 1797 it was occupied by Benjamin Jesty, the pioneer of smallpox vaccination. Partial rebuilding in 1906 by Guy Montague Marston, gave the house its present appearance. The artist George Spencer-Watson purchased the manor in 1923 and lived here until his death in 1934, after which it passed to his daughter Mary, the noted sculptress. She was the last occupant of the manor and, after she died in 2006, the building fell into disrepair.

Recently it was acquired by the Landmark Trust who are carrying out essential work in order to make it habitable.

When I visited Dunshay, with the kind permission of the site manager, I was to discover a beautiful, but dilapidated, overgrown and mystical place which is a spark to the imagination.

The front of the manor has two gables with the main entrance set back between them. All of the windows are small, stone framed with mullions. The gateway, though lacking gates is flanked by a pair of tall, rectangular pillars, each surmounted by a steeple. A stepped mounting block stands to one side and all fronted by a large, impressive, circular ornamental pond with a stone balustrade.

To the left is a magnificent long barn with, I believe, an integral cottage.

Dunshay Barn

Dunshay is one of the most secluded and magical places I have found on Purbeck.

Furzebrook

Situated just to the south of Stoborough, Furzebrook is not a village as one expects.

Like Harman's Cross, it does not have a church, shop or pub and exists mainly because of the fine clay found in the area.

A mile long road, edged with residential dwellings leads to a large, operational clay works, Furzebrook House and a modern village hall. These are sited in a landscape dotted with numerous, disused and mainly flooded clay-pits. Although a little isolated, the Village Hall is very popular. With excellent facilities, it is often rented out for functions and performances by groups and societies from quite far afield.

In 1780, Furzebrook House was purchased by the Pike brothers as the headquarters of their clay-mining empire. In recent years it passed to the Institute of Terrestrial Ecology whose responsibility was to preserve the countryside and farming of Purbeck and surrounding areas. At present, it is in private ownership but is in a rather neglected and dilapidated condition.

Furzebrook House

Many visitors come to Furzebrook as it is there they will find one of Purbeck's best known attractions, the Blue Pool. Originally a clay pit, this huge hole has since filled with water.

The lake covers three acres, is fifty feet deep and surrounded by dense woodland. With a high concentration of minerals, the water does not support any vegetation or animal life. Clay particles in the lake cause it to change colour from blue, turquoise or shades of green, dependant on weather and light.

The Blue Pool

In 1935, it was bought by Capt. T.T. Barnard, who developed the lake as a beauty spot, laying paths, steps and building a Tea House. This long, low building incorporates a museum which, through artifacts and dioramas,

shows the history of local clay mining. One wing is a gift shop which is also the home of the Wareham Bears. These miniature teddies are exhibited in models showing them at work, play and relaxing at home.

The Tea House

East and West Holme

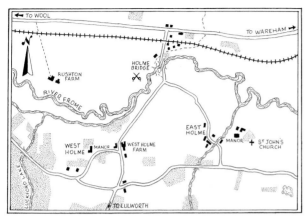

Leaving the main thoroughfare from Wareham to Wool, the road to Lulworth passes across an unmanned level crossing and a bridge over the River Frome. Alongside this fairly modern construction stands the original 17th century, six-arched Holme Bridge. The history of this bridge makes it worth a visit for it is the site of a little known, small but gallant battle of the English Civil War. On 27th February 1644, a Parliamentary force of 300 men, under the command of Capt. Francis Sydenham, arrived at the bridge to find it defended by just 45 Royalist soldiers of Lord Inchiquins Irish Regiment. During the ensuing battle, their commander, Capt. Purdon, though wounded, encouraged his men to stand. They bravely did so, holding off the Roundheads for five hours. When Irish reinforcements arrived, Sydenham withdrew, leaving 40 of his men dead. Purdon's force suffered only 12 wounded and 1 fatality. Musket balls from the fight are still occasionally found in the river bed and surrounding fields.

Holme Bridge

Approximately two hundred yards from the bridge, a lane on the left takes the visitor into the tiny, picture postcard hamlet of East Holme.

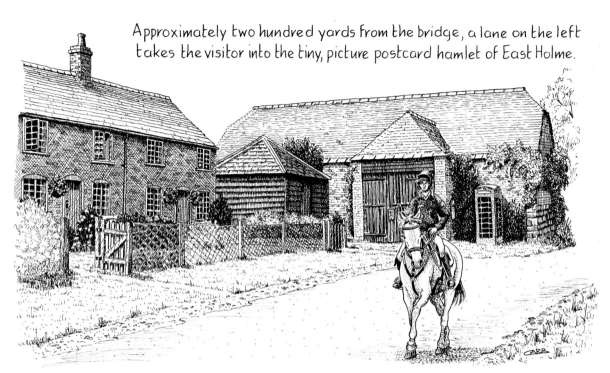

East Holme

The settlement grew around the site of a 12th century Cluniac Priory established by Robert de Lincoln, a Norman knight.

In the centre, a large barn and a grain store on 'mushroom' plinths stands at the end of a terrace of gardened cottages. Opposite, in front of a large, Victorian style house is a well tended, grassy hummock on which sits an antique, commemorative hand-operated water pump.

Exit to the south is via a ford, after which, a lane to the left leads to the Priory House and the church.

Water Pump

Holme Priory House

Crest of the Bond Family

The Priory has long gone, even though, after the Dissolution, it continued as the parish church until 1715.

On its footings now stands Holme Priory House, a fine manor initially built by Nathaniel Bond in 1770, no doubt utilising materials from the ruins of the Priory. It was extended and refurbished between 1790 and 1865 by three subsequent Nathaniels. Priory Farm, behind the manor is also an 18th century building, again making use of the convenient source of stone. The original chancel arch from the Priory was also recycled by Dennis Bond in 1849 who re-erected it in his chapel at Creech Grange.

I have been told that Holme Priory House is still occupied by the Bond family.

Church of Saint John

The fourth Nathaniel also built a new place of worship in 1866, the small church of St John the Evangelist. Situated a few yards to the east of the house, it was designed by John Hicks of Dorchester, for whom Thomas Hardy worked from 1856 until 1862.

It is one of Hicks' more elaborate churches, built from dark brown heathstone and is a fine example of Victorian religious taste.

The painted decoration inside the church was done by Lady Selina Bond who:- *"with her own hands adorned these walls".*

In the porch is a Certificate of Merit which states that the church has been:- *"Sympathetically maintained as part of the landscape".*

The lane which runs through East Holme terminates at the road which runs westward towards Wool alongside the border of the military firing ranges. After half a mile, it passes over a crossroads and the road to Lulworth. Turning right you enter the few buildings which make up West Holme.

Holme Farm and Garden Centre

This hamlet is well known for the farm with its first class Garden Centre, shop, café and pick-your-own facilities.
Opposite the entrance gate is the 17th century West Holme House, an architecturally interesting building.

West Holme House

West Holme Manor

The lane to the left of Holme House takes you past West Holme Manor and Farm, the latter also catering for guests. The estate originally belonged to the Norman knight Walter de Clavile of Church Knowle.

Beyond the fields of the farm, in the danger area of the ranges and through dense woodland, runs a stream, rather oddly named 'Luckford Lake'. Its gently flowing waters have a geographical importance. Rising on Povington Hill, it runs to join the River Frome near Holme Bridge and marks the western boundary of the Isle of Purbeck.

Luckford Lake

Stoborough

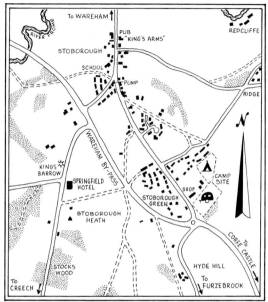

From Wareham's south bridge, spanning the River Frome, the road enters the Isle of Purbeck via a causeway which crosses the water meadows to Stoborough within the parish of Arne.

This village sits in the north-west corner of the heathlands which run almost unbroken to the coast at Studland. At one time the heath was hated by some, who believed it to harbour radicals and dissenters.

Access to the village is gained between a garage and an attractive pub, with a few cottages close by.

Very few of the buildings are older than the 18th century, and the further you travel up the road the more modern they become.

The reason for this is that, in 1643, during the Civil War, the population burned the village to the ground. This was to deny occupation by any Royalist forces who might threaten the Parliamentary garrison at Wareham.

It seems very peculiar that a community who supported Cromwell should name the village pub, when rebuilt, 'The King's Arms'.

The King's Arms

Thatched cottages by the green

The burning of the original houses may also be
the reason that, unusually for Dorset, there are
very few buildings in Stoborough with thatched
roofs. There is no church in the village but a
small housing in the corner of the triangular
green contains the old water pump and is also
the War Memorial.

At the upper end of the village there is a large
caravan site with a shop.

Pump Housing

On the western fringe of Stoborough, just off the road to Creech, is a lovely, white house called 'King's Barrow.' The name of the property derives from a large Bronze Age burial mound which rises within its grounds.

Originally measuring about 65 feet in diameter and 12 feet high, the tomb was excavated in 1767. It was found to contain a 10 foot by 4 foot oak coffin made from a hollow tree. In the casket was a headless skeleton sewn up in a deerskin. With it was a small piece of gold filigree and a drinking cup made of oak or shale.

King's Barrow

The quality of these items point to the interred body being that of a man of importance, perhaps even a 'King'.

The mound is possibly the origin of the name Stoborough, for the settlement is recorded in Domesday Book as 'Stanberge' meaning *Stony Hill* or *Barrow.* It may be that the name of the village pub also refers to the buried 'king'.

At one time the barrow must have been a striking landmark but, over the passing centuries, Mother Nature has shielded it from sight. Dense woodland, a tangled web of rhododendrons and a thick carpet of leaves make it difficult to find. It was only through the generous guidance of the owner that I was able to have a look at this piece of Purbeck history. I must stress that King's Barrow is private property and there is no public access.

The Barrow

Stoborough Heath

To the east of the village, behind the caravan park, Stoborough Heath was once home to people who were at the opposite end of the social ladder to the 'king'.

These heathcroppers were a despised group who eked out a living from this rough terrain, trading in peat, furze, bacon and corn. They were known locally as 'nesseltripes'.

The heath is now a National Nature Reserve and its inauguration as such is marked by a large cairn close to its eastern fringe, just above the 'Soldier's Road'. (I have never before seen so many Adders in one place.)

National Nature Reserve Cairn

142

Ridge and Pikes Tramway

The small residential development of Ridge lies east of Stoborough and is part of the parish of Arne. It is located south of the tidal River Frome which winds its way through water meadows to enter Poole Harbour and marks the northern boundary of the Isle of Purbeck.

The hamlet has few amenities other than a pair of farms, each with a camp site and two sailing clubs with wharfs.

Barnhill Road, Ridge

The houses, mainly built in the 20th century, stand on a site once occupied by Powell's Cement Works which operated there between 1874 and 1922, during which time it boasted five Bottle Kilns.

The chalk and marl required for the process was brought to the factory by horse drawn carts from a quarry near Church Knowle.

Bottle Kiln

Sailing Club at Redcliffe

The flat landscape of water meadows to the north and heathlands to the south are only broken by the 45 foot high Redcliffe. This tree-shrouded precipice of red sand and clay sits above a sharp bend in the river, three quarters of a mile south-east of Wareham. Its bulk shelters a yacht club, farm and campsite from the wind.

The River Frome near Ridge was once renowned for its high population of eels, the trapping of which provided some local fishermen with a good source of income. Sadly, their numbers have declined in recent years.

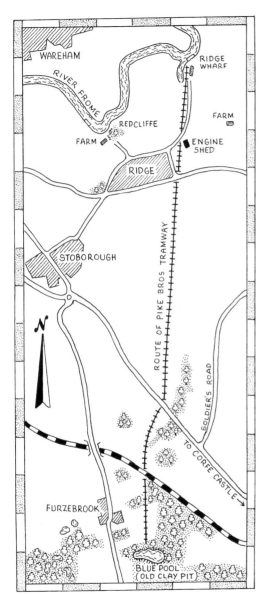

In 1780, the Pike brothers of Devon set up a clay mining operation based at Furzebrook. Amongst their many quarries, the largest was the fifty foot deep hole, now filled with water and known to visitors as the 'Blue Pool.'

In order to transport the clay, they built a straight road for horse-drawn carts from Furzebrook across the heath to the wharf at Ridge.

By 1886, this was converted into a narrow gauge railway with a steam locomotive named 'Primus'. Through the years, engines were replaced, 'Primus' being followed by 'Secundus', 'Tertius', 'Quartus', 'Quintus', up to 'Septimus' in 1930. All have long been scrapped except for the rebuilt 'Secundus' which is on display at the Corfe Castle Railway Museum. In 1954, the engines were changed to diesel until the tramway finally closed in 1970.

'Quintus'

145

The old railway line has been adapted as a Public Footpath and provides an excellent walking route from 'Blue Pool' across the heath to emerge at Ridge.

Route of Pike's Tramway

Engine Shed

The Engine Shed, now derelict, once housed Pikes' locomotives. Plans are now under discussion to refurbish the building by the volunteers from the Norden Mining Museum.

Ridge Wharf

Now a large boating centre, this was once the embarkation point where barges were loaded with clay for shipment to Poole.

Beneath the modern jetty can be seen some of the rotting timber pilings which supported the original wharf.

Arne ~ 'a Saxon quiet place'

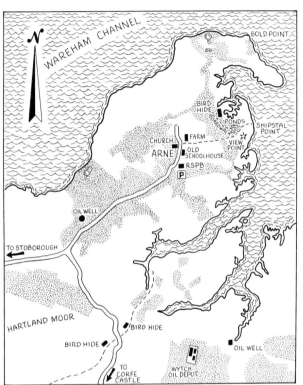

The northern shore of Purbeck, opening on to Poole Harbour, consists of a huge heath-covered peninsula. At its centre, on a low hill, is the tiny hamlet of Arne, surrounded by some of the few fields to be found in the parish.

Originally belonging to the Abbey of Shaftesbury, the name comes from the Saxon words 'aenne' or 'aern' which means 'house' or 'secret place'.

A common sight on the peninsula, especially in the early morning and evenings, is scores of Roe Deer. They are very used to human contact and, with care, are very approachable.

If lucky, you may spot the rarer Sika Deer which, having been introduced to Brownsea Island in 1896, have migrated to Arne.

Roe Deer

Besides its wildlife and natural beauty, Arne is also famous as the home of the first on-shore oil drilling development based at Wytch Farm.

RSPB Information Centre

Arne is a Nature Reserve and, on the approach to the village is a car park and Information Centre run by the RSPB. The reserve covers some 12,000 acres across which is a network of paths which take you over heathland, through woods and to the coastal areas

Dartford Warbler

There is a lookout point on a large mound which offers wonderful views over the harbour and Purbeck countryside. Birdlife is abundant and you can observe breeds such as the Linnet, Yellow Hammer, Hawks and the rare Dartford Warbler.

Church of Saint Nicholas of Myra.

Perched on a gentle slope above the road close to the farm is the heavily buttressed, 13th century church of Saint Nicholas. First built as a chantry, it is small and plain, having no tower, just a chancel and nave under one roof, with a south porch.

The medieval altar, with five incised crosses, has a beautiful green frontal depicting eight sea vessels in silver, from a warship of Alfred the Great to a modern car ferry. Completed in 1989, this embroidery was created by Kirsten Webb of Stoborough. Behind the altar, a triptic window offers a wonderful view across the harbour. Three yachts appear on the pulpit fall and represent the Holy Trinity, whilst the anchor on the priest's vestment is one of the oldest forms of the cross. Near the south door are traces of early wall paintings which show that the church was once highly decorated until the puritanical Cromwell had them whitewashed over.

Across the road from the church are two brick-built cottages. At one time they served as the schoolhouse. The original building opened as a school in 1832, but was rebuilt as it now stands, by Lord Eldon in 1874. Unfortunately, due to a fall in the number of pupils, it closed as a school in 1922. They were turned into private houses and today are leased out as holiday homes.

The Old Schoolhouse

At the farm the road takes a right-hand turn where it becomes a bridleway which runs through the Nature Reserve to the coast at Shipstal Point. Where it terminates, a set of steps lead down to one of the loveliest, and secret beaches on Purbeck. This gorgeous sweep of sand is backed by a 300 metre stretch of cliffs and is littered with oyster shells.

During WWII, Arne was lit up as a decoy to draw enemy bombers away from the munitions factory at Holton Lee. An anti-aircraft gun was sited on Shipstal Point.

Shipstal Point

Dragonfly and Insect Ponds

The habitats of Arne are very diverse as is the wildlife which occupy them. When walking the paths, be sure to look out for squirrels, rabbits, spiders and the occasional huge ant hills. From the bridleway, below the lookout hill, a track passes through an area of freshwater marsh in which Gypsywort, Wild Celery and Yellow Iris flourish. Damsel and Dragonflies whirr across the larger ponds which are also home to a multitude of insects and reptiles.

Four-Spotted Chaser Dragonfly

Big Wood and the Boardwalk

Whether a lover of beauty or nature, visitors never tire of walking round the Arne Reserve. Having enjoyed the views from the lookout hill and passed by the ponds, the path enters Big Wood. Traversing this somewhat boggy area has been made easier by the efforts of the RSPB who have built an excellent boardwalk across the roughest parts.

Until a few years ago, parts of the wood were overgrown by invasive rhododendron bushes. The land management team put in a lot of effort to clear most of these and open up the areas between the trees.

Twitchers and the heathlands

Bird Hide
in
Big Wood

It is not surprising that Arne, with its woods, marshes, creeks and heathlands has become a mecca for ornithologists. Under its careful management, the RSPB has catered very well for these telescope and camera wielding enthusiasts. As well as establishing the bird-life centre by the village, the organisation maintains the excellent system of pathways, boardwalks, viewing points and bird-hides in the nature reserve.

The largest bird-hide has three floors and stands on the shoreline of Big Wood and overlooks Poole Harbour and Arne Bay.

A coastal path running south from Shipstal Point is very popular with birdwatchers. With plenty of viewing points from which to observe sea-birds on the salt marshes and across Wytch Channel to Long and Round Islands

Shepherds Hut Bird Hide

Birdwatchers

South-west of the village, Hartland Moor is another favoured place for ornithologists.
Either side of the road to Norden, on a cross track, are two bird-hides converted from old, wheeled shepherds huts. They offer shelter and some comfort in bad weather.

View over Hartland Moor

The great heathlands which dominate the area around Arne are a unique habitat for other varieties of wildlife which merit their status as a Site of Special Scientific Interest (SSSI). Here can be found all six species of British Reptiles, including the Sand Lizard and Smooth Snake, both endangered and protected by law.

The whole of the Parish of Arne is a delight in all seasons and the perfect place to wander in fine weather. On a misty or rain sodden day, the moors and heaths take on a brooding atmosphere, only heightened by occasional glimpses of the jagged silhouette of Corfe Castle in the blue tinted hills of the central Purbeck ridge. This open landscape well deserves its reputation as a place of beauty, solitude, peace and tranquillity.

Corfe Castle from Hartland Moor

POSTSCRIPT

As with most of the county, Purbeck continues to develop in order to suit modern requirements. However, with conservation a prime necessity, most of the new buildings and attractions are sympathetically designed to complement the landscape and do not detract from the beauty and mystique of the island. Kimmeridge has a new Village Hall which incorporates a wonderful Fossil Museum, whilst the landlord of the Square and Compass at Worth has constructed an intriguing timber henge near the car park. In Swanage, the modern Lifeboat Station is nearing completion.

In this book I have but scratched the surface of the Isle of Purbeck, leaving much more for visitors to discover for themselves in this lovely part of Dorset.